This Journal Belongs To:

_____

_____

Copyright © 2021 by Sami Volinski
All rights reserved.

Without your voice we don't exist.
Please, support us and leave a review

Thank you!

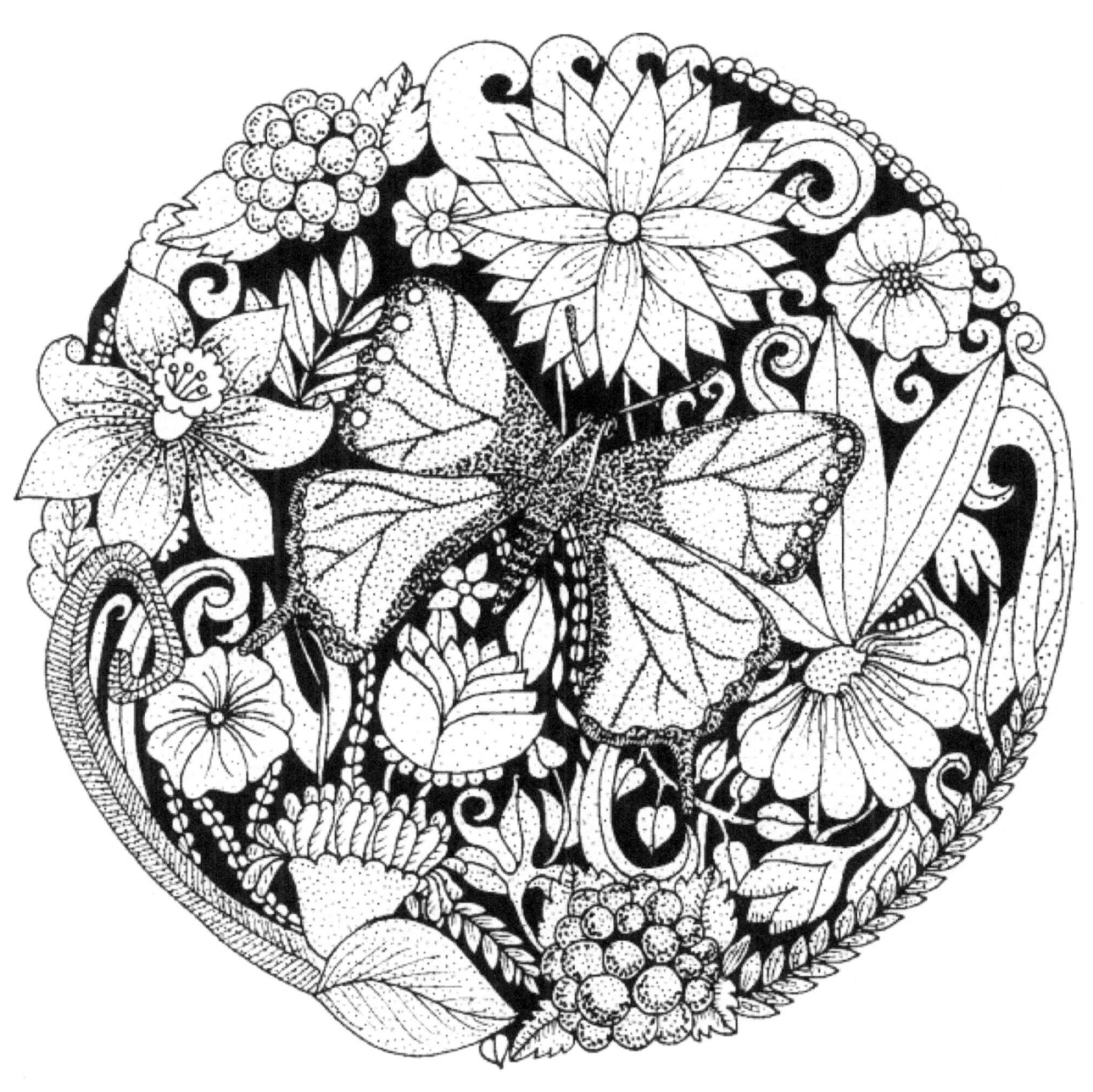

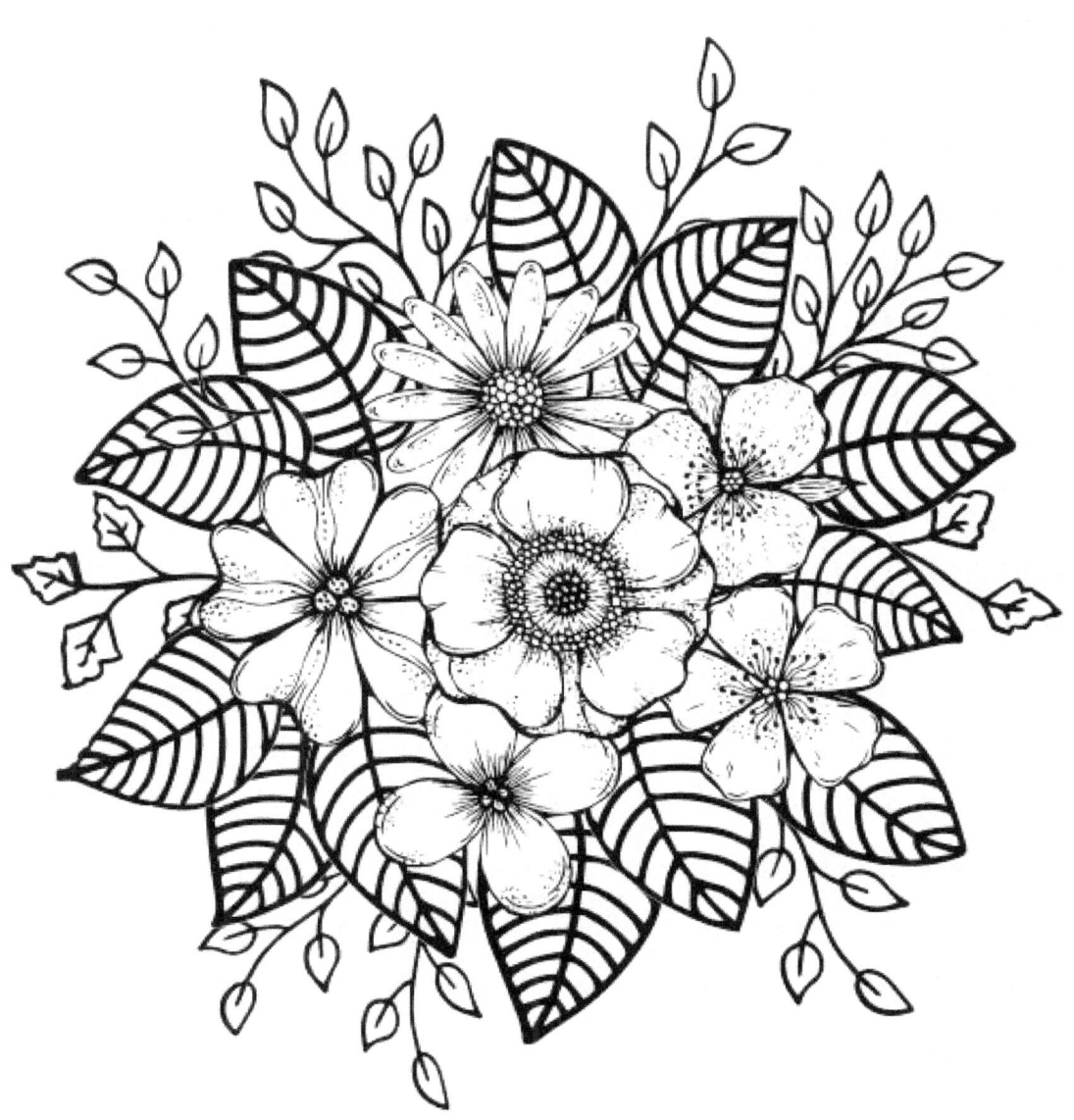

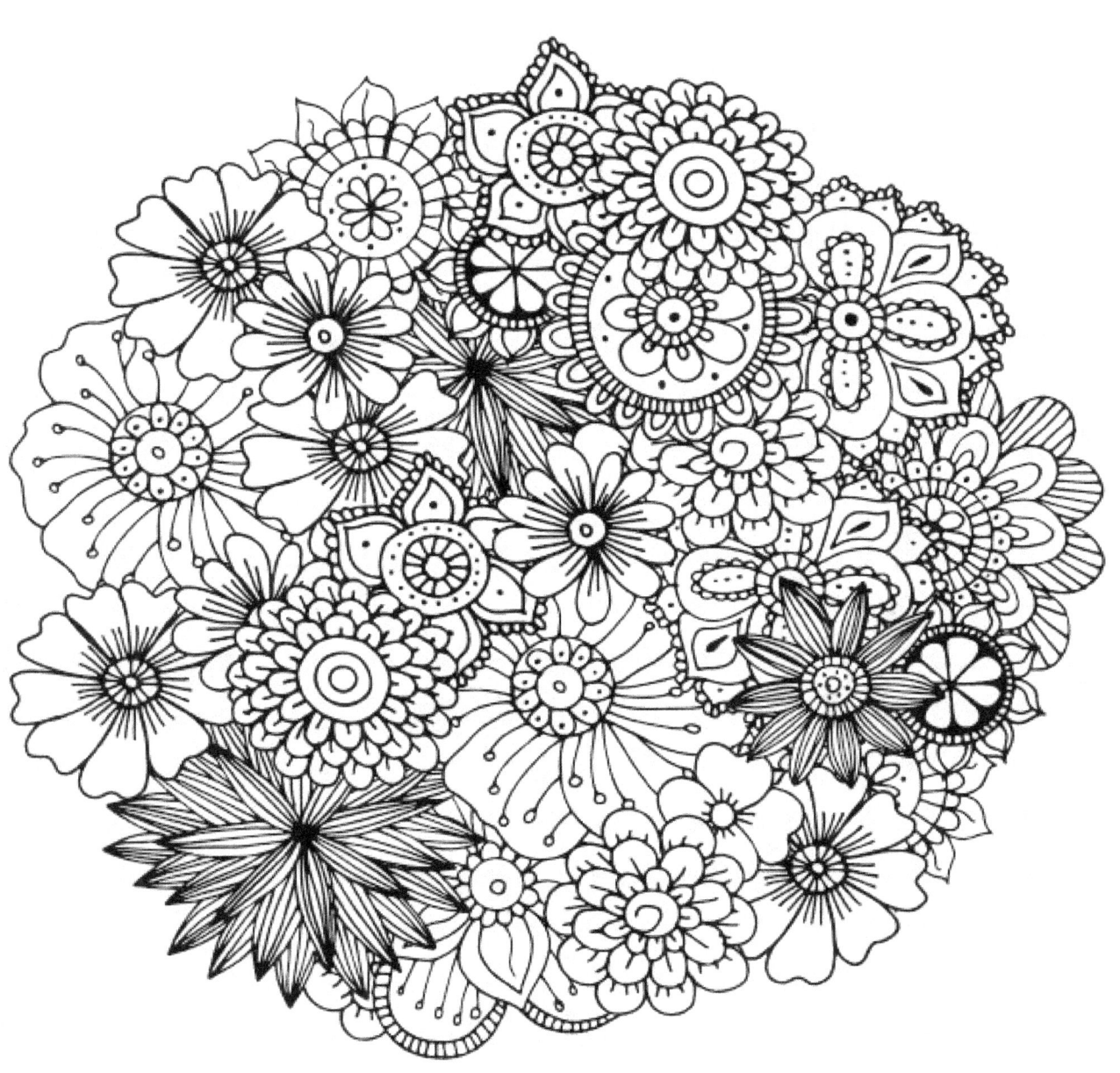

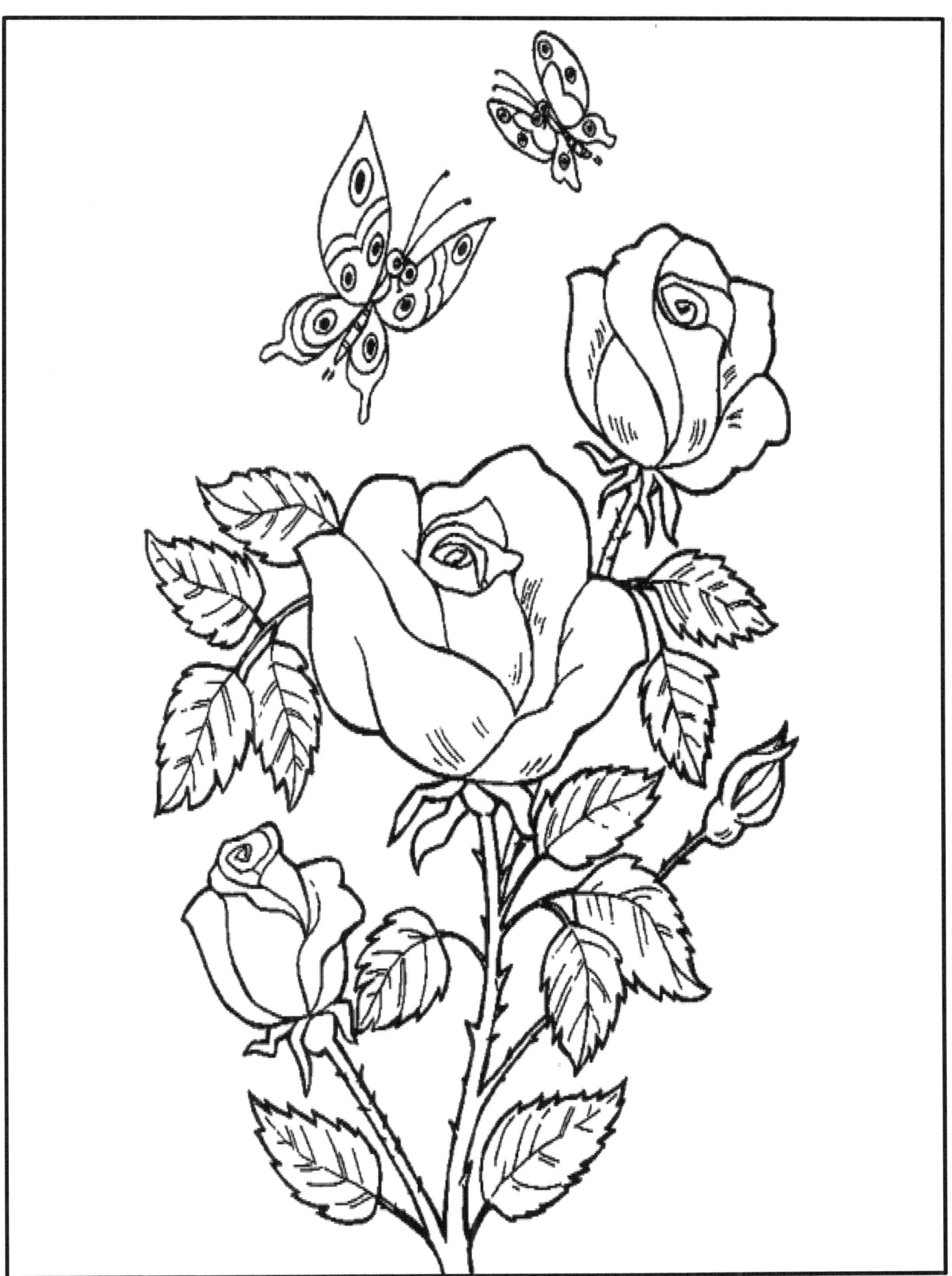

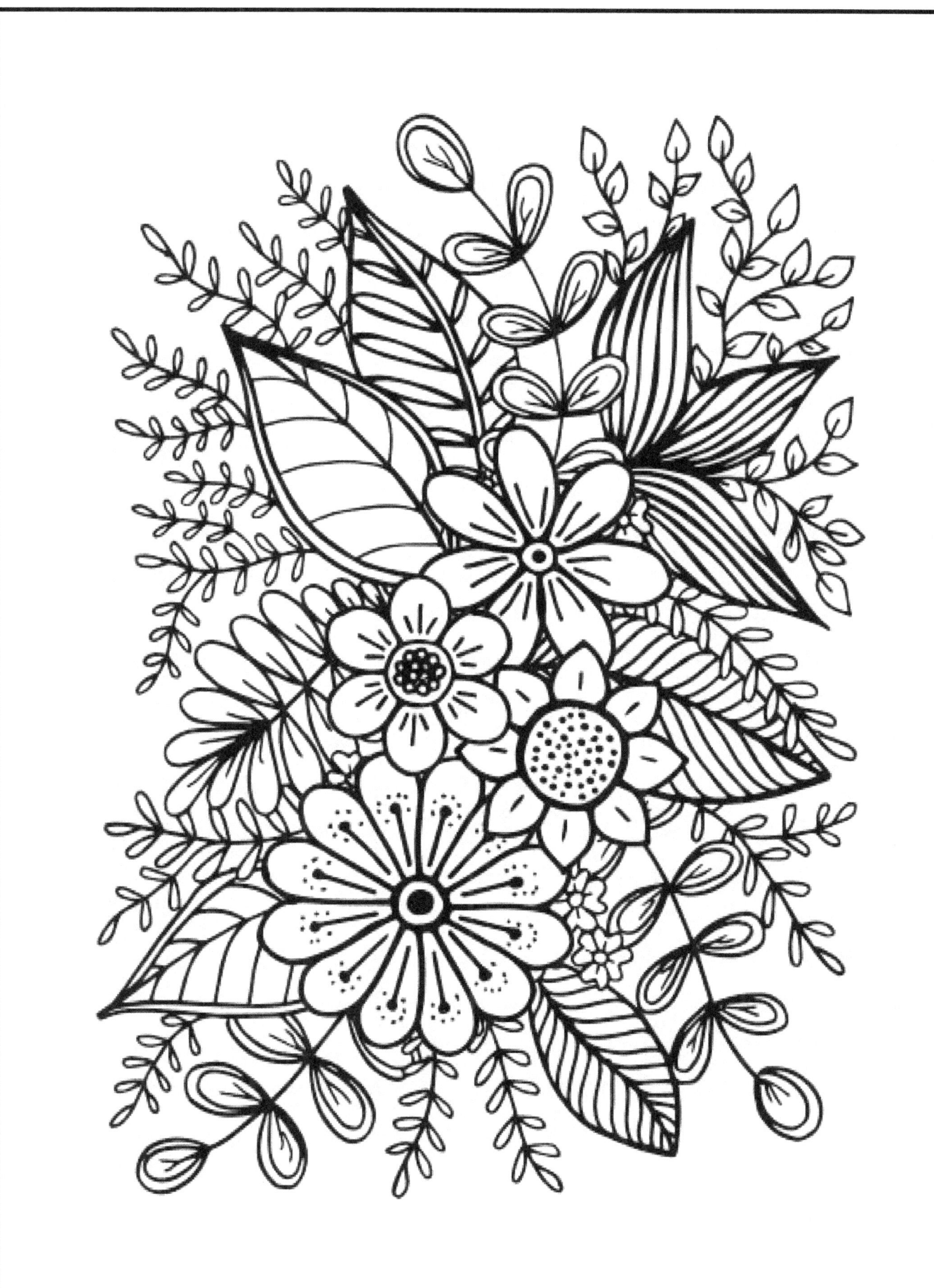

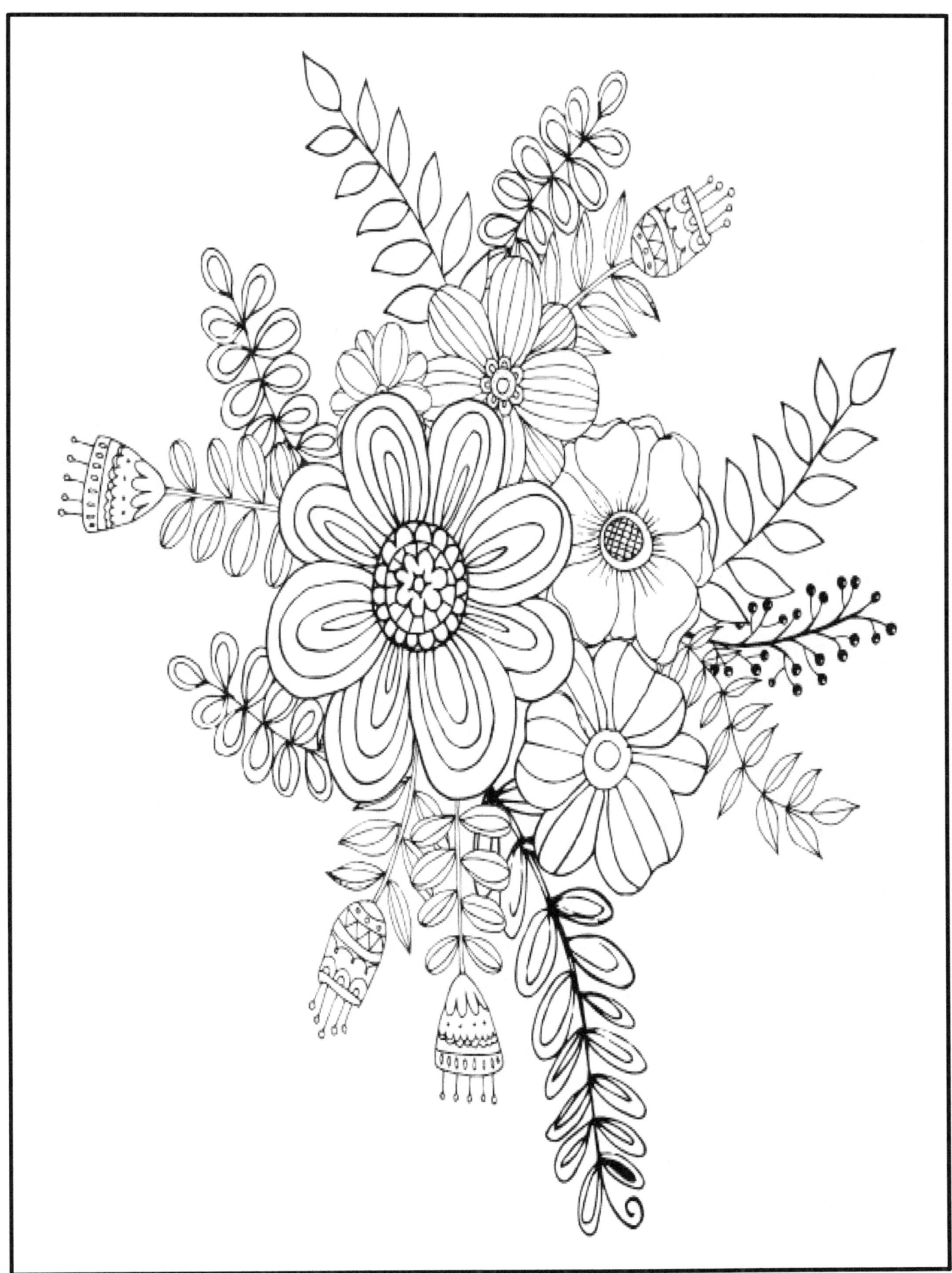

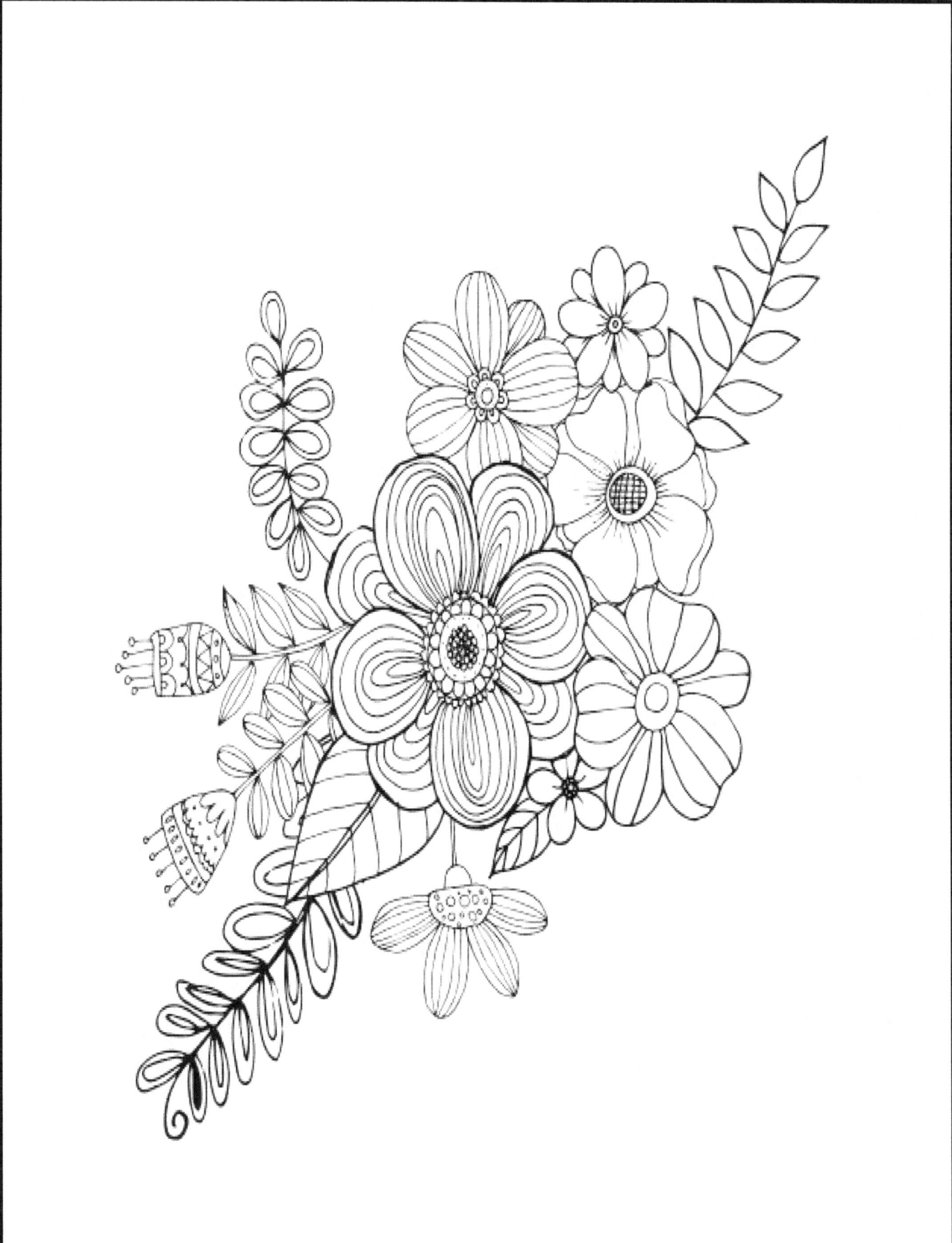

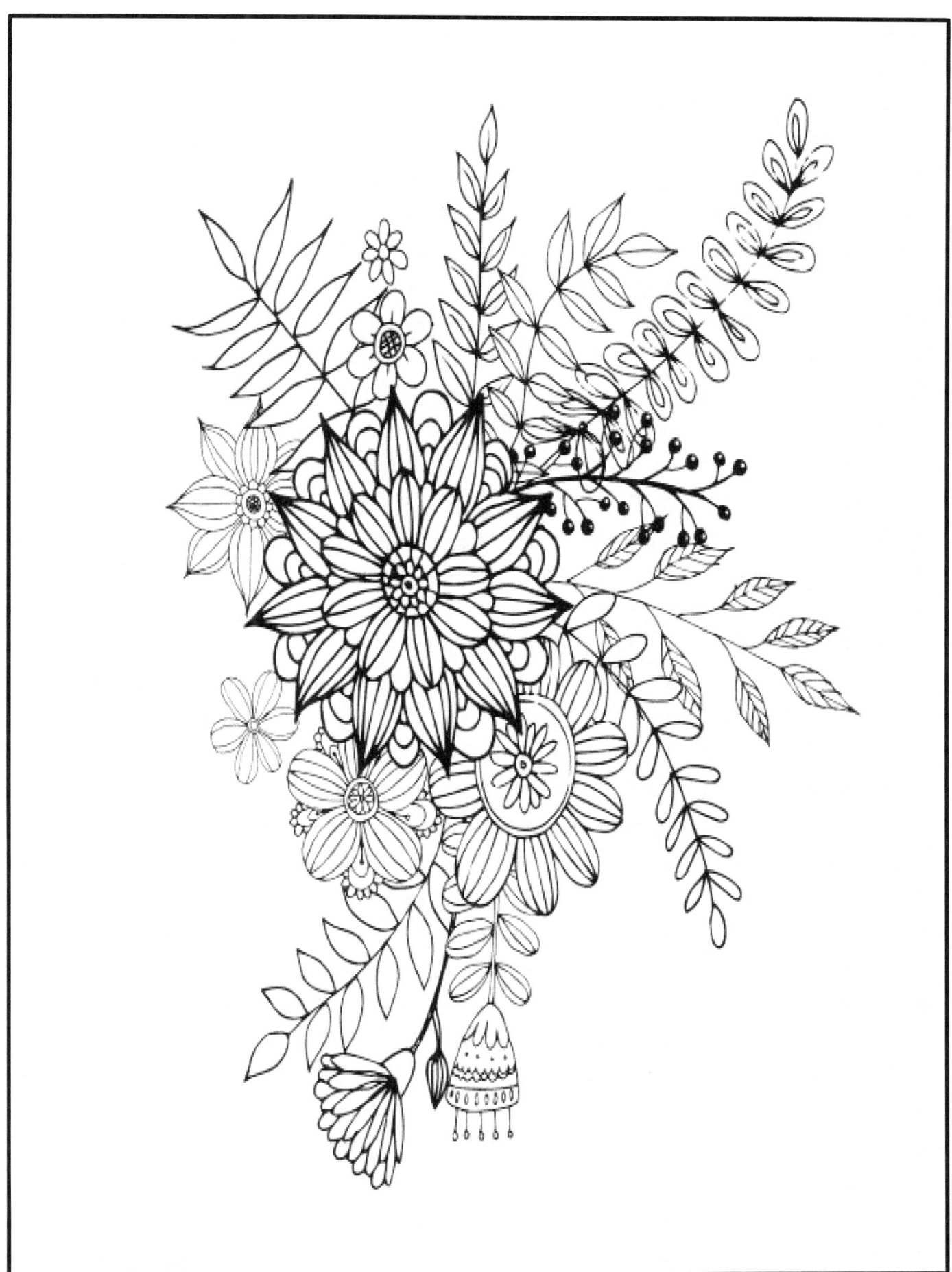

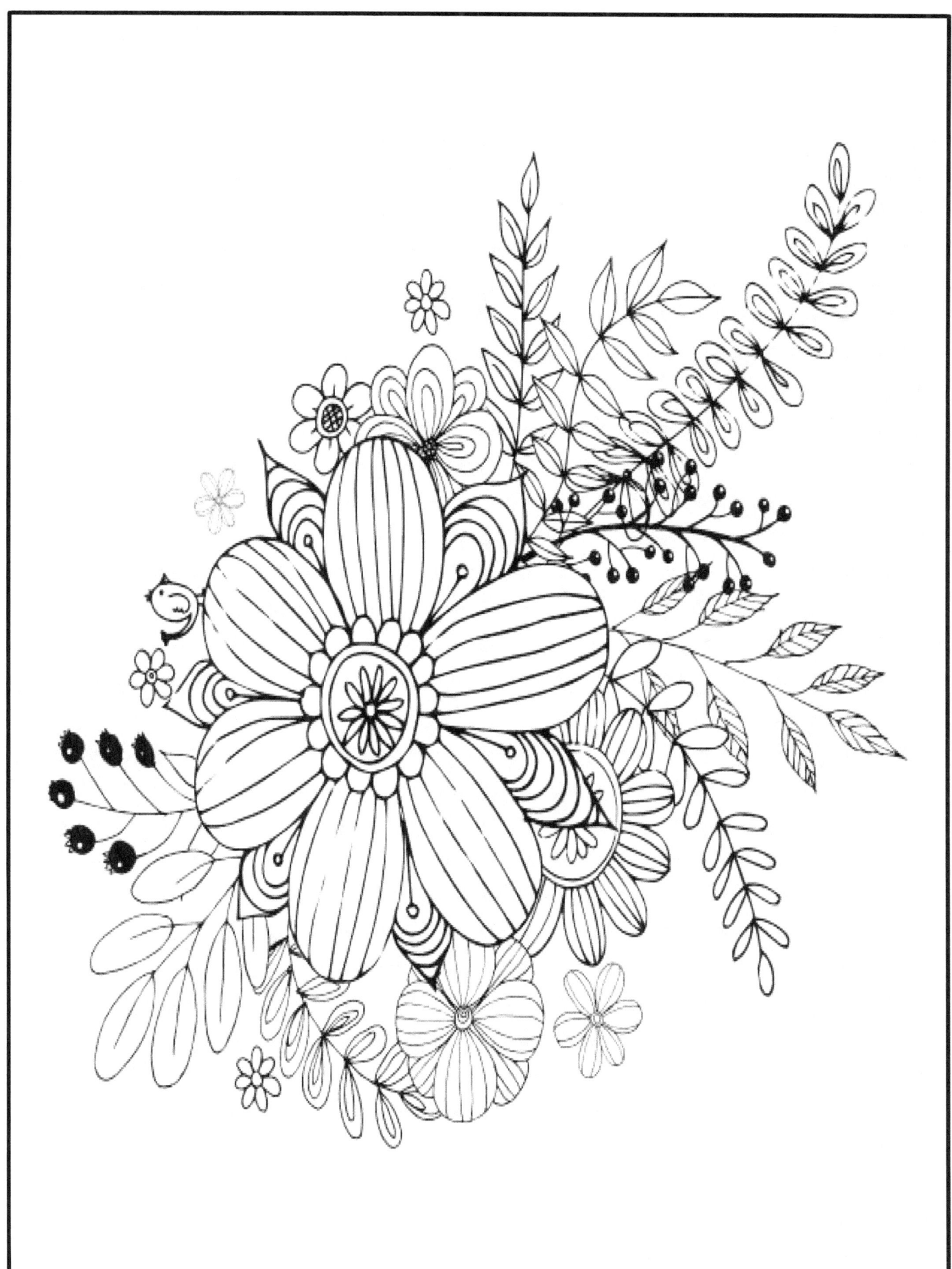

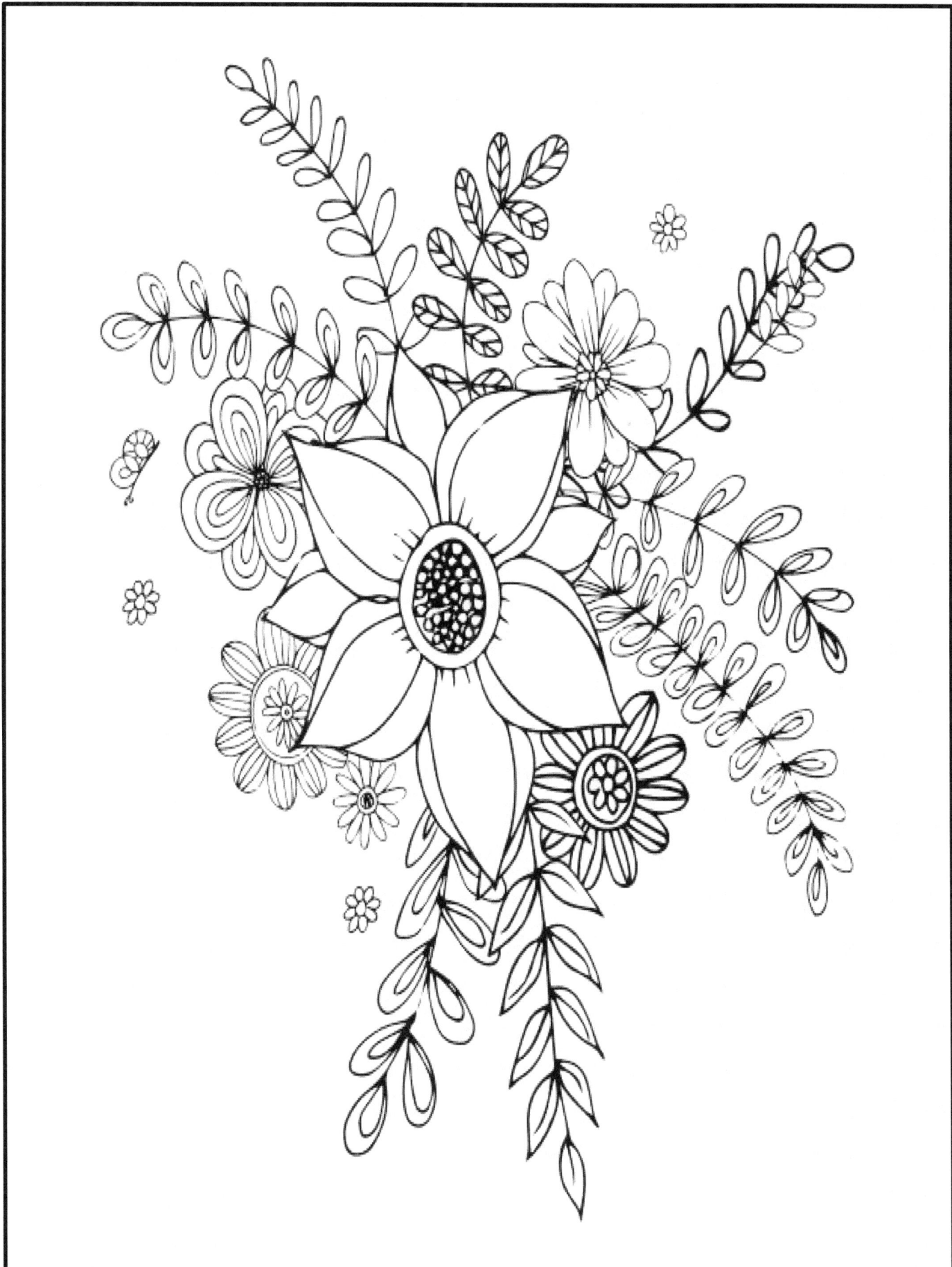

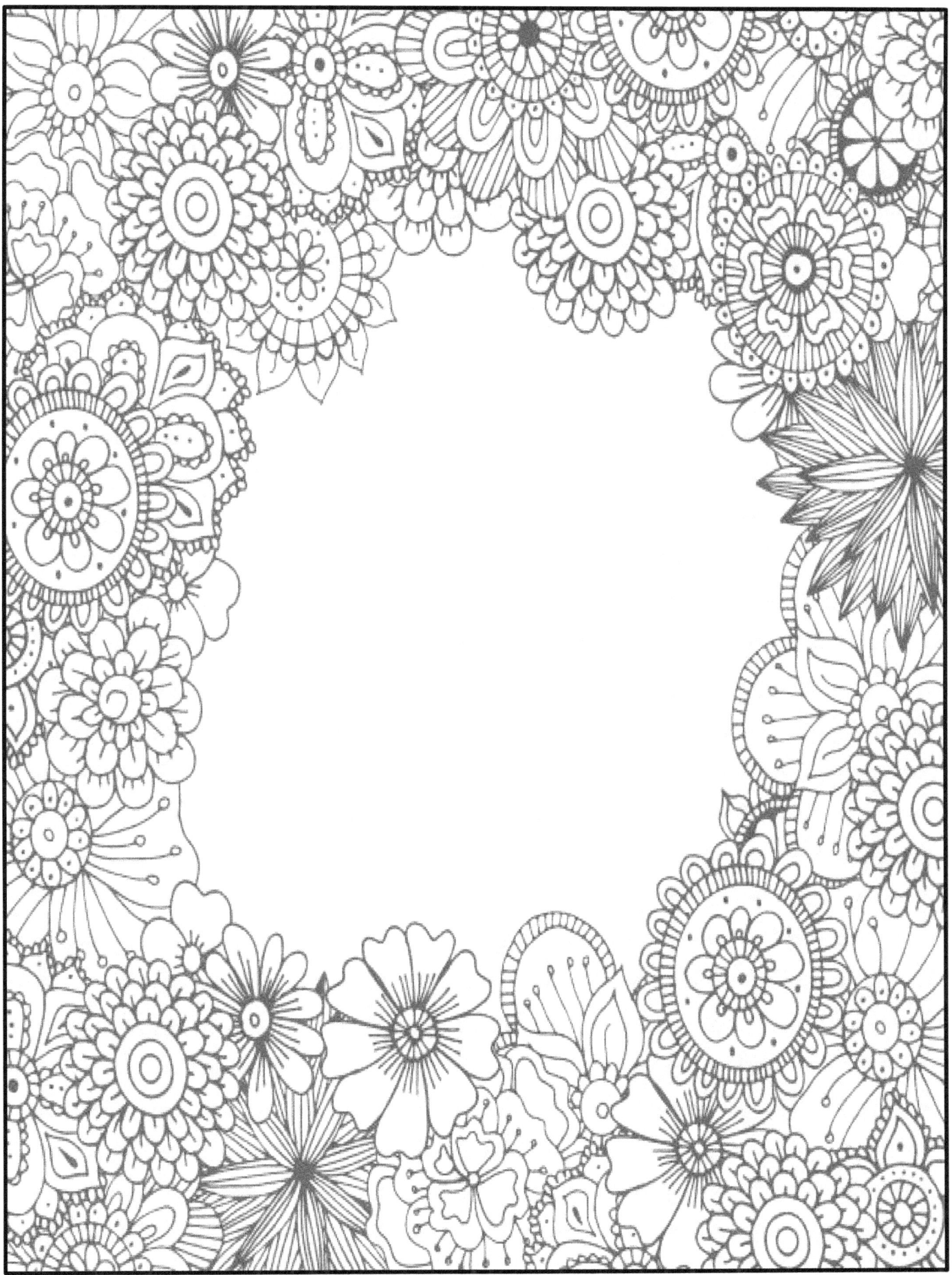

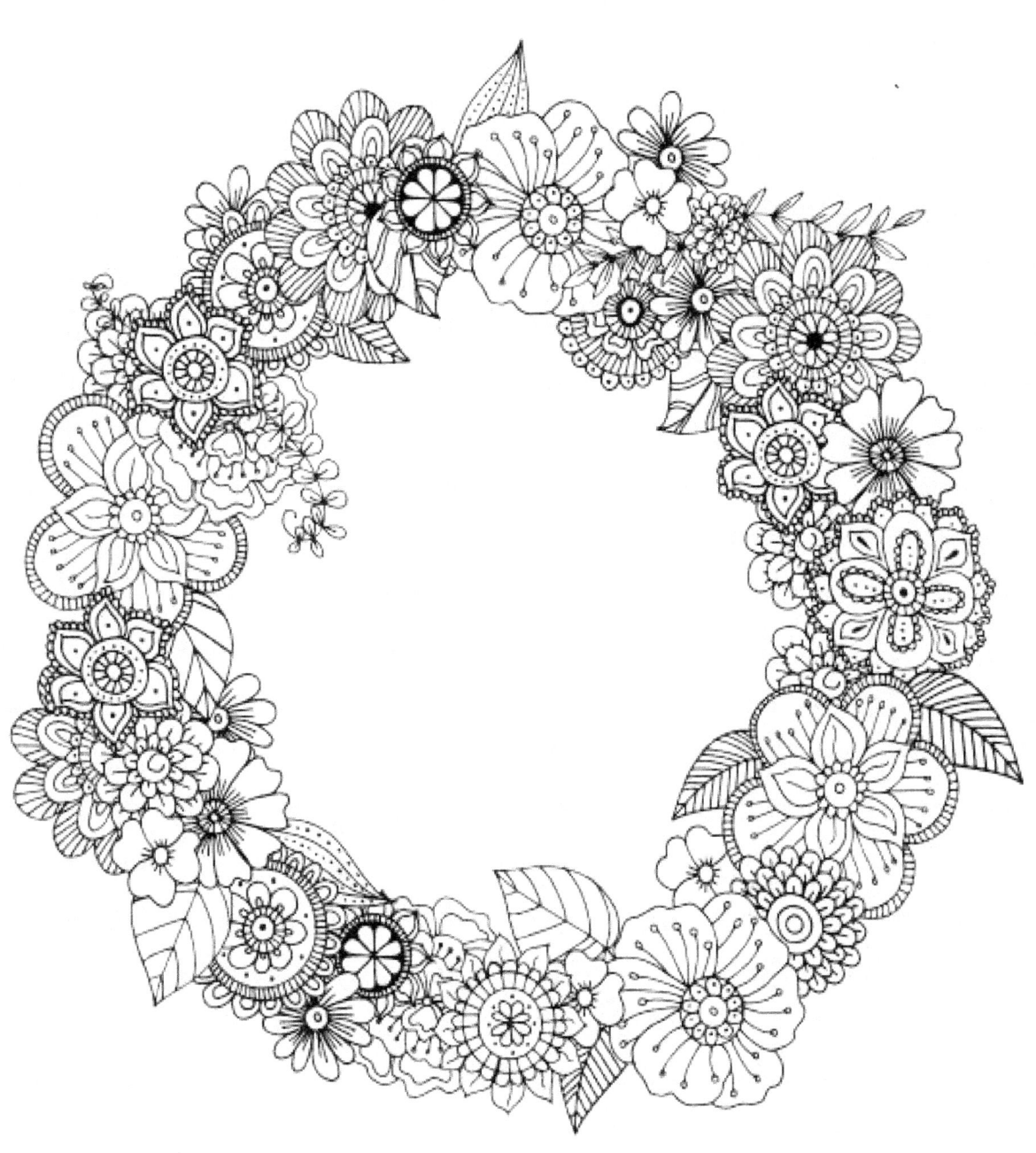

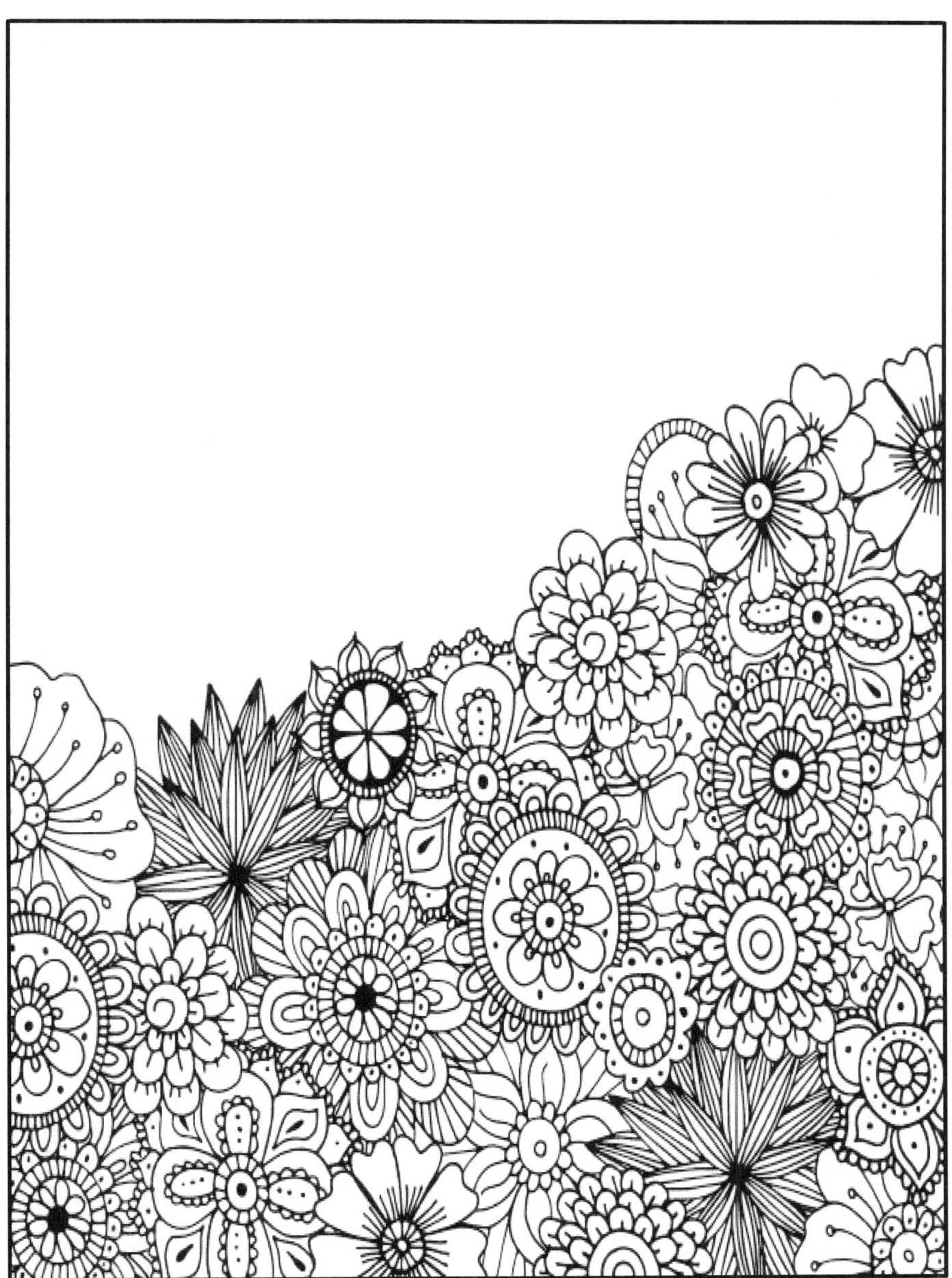

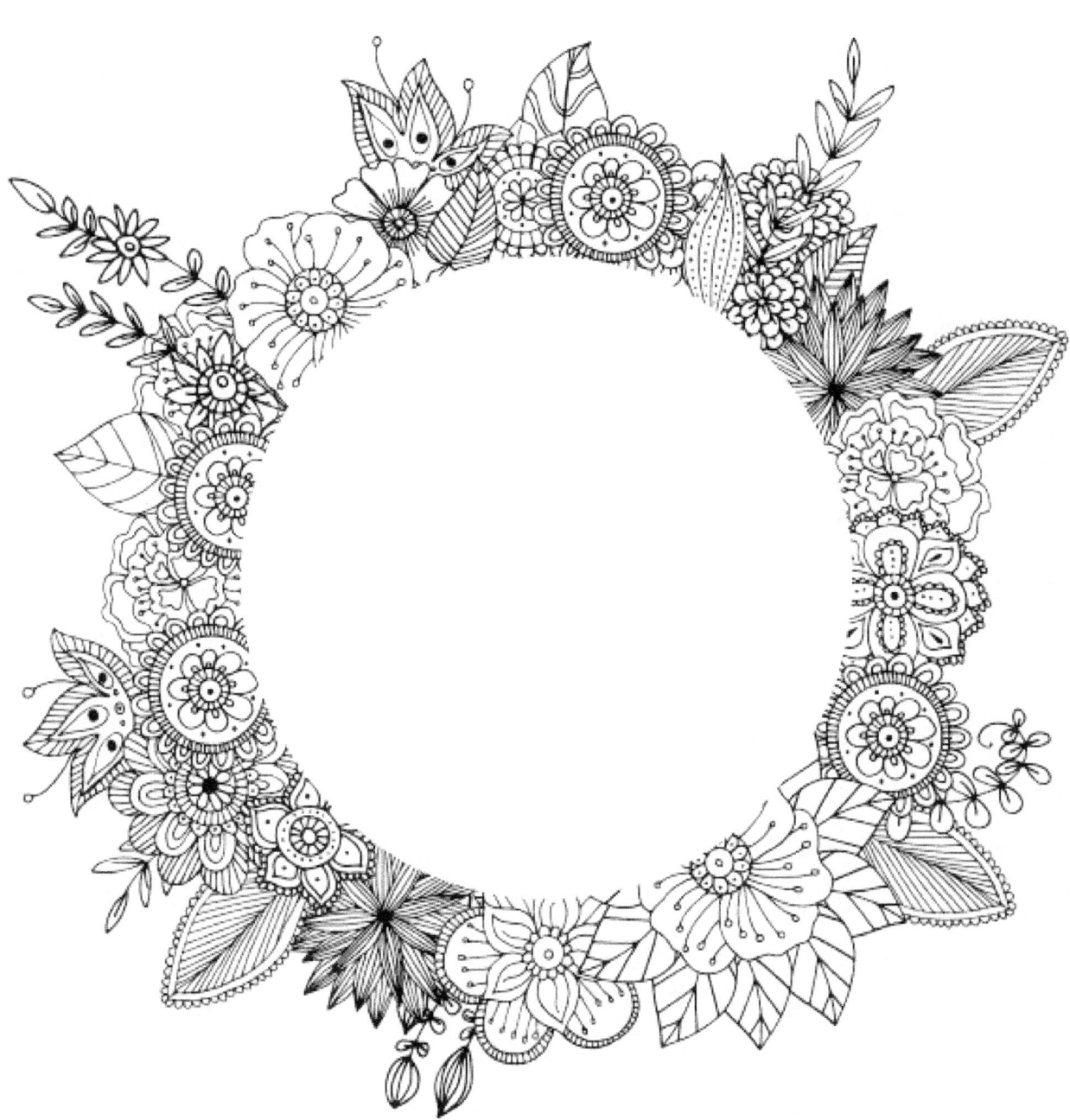

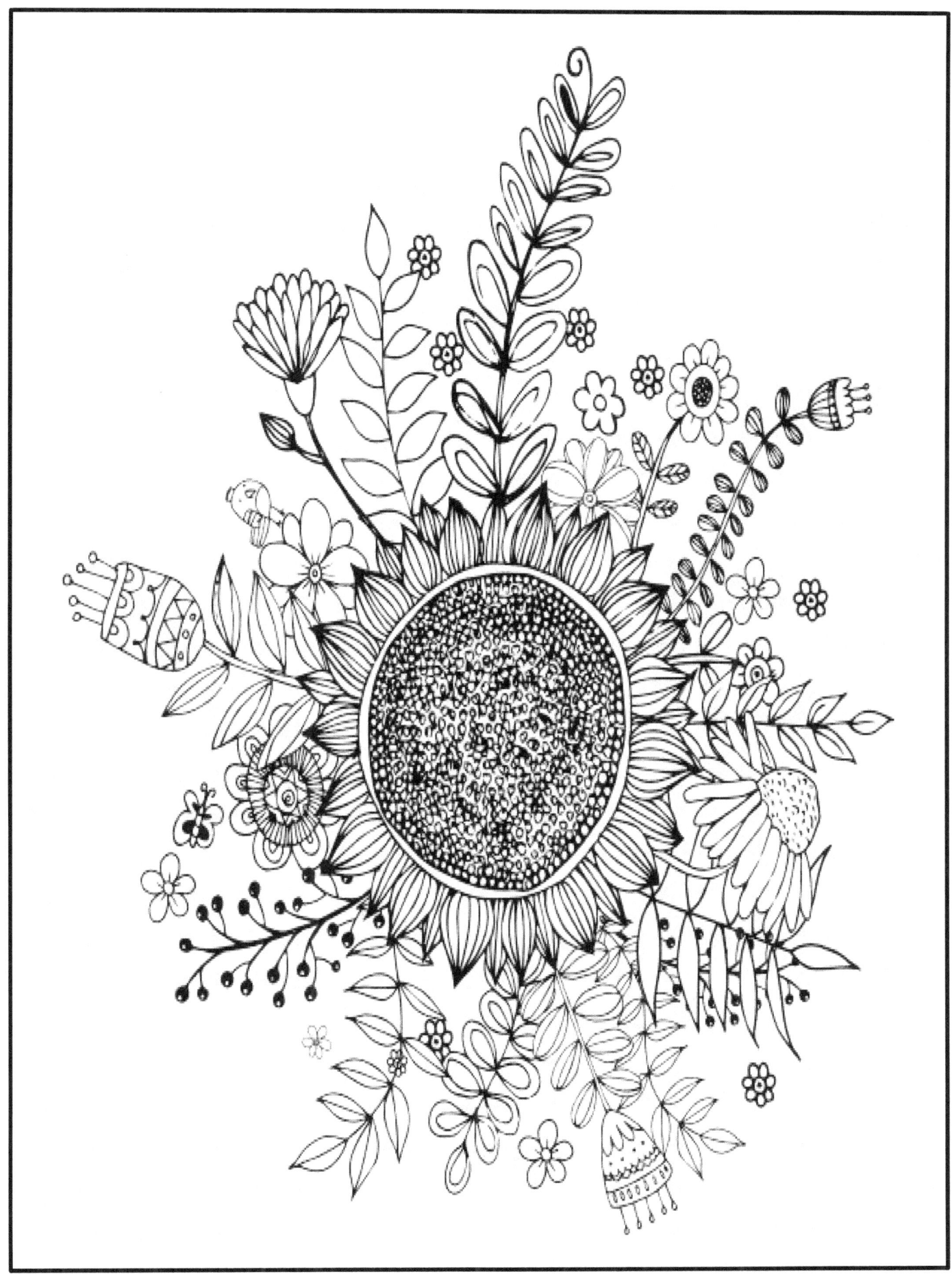

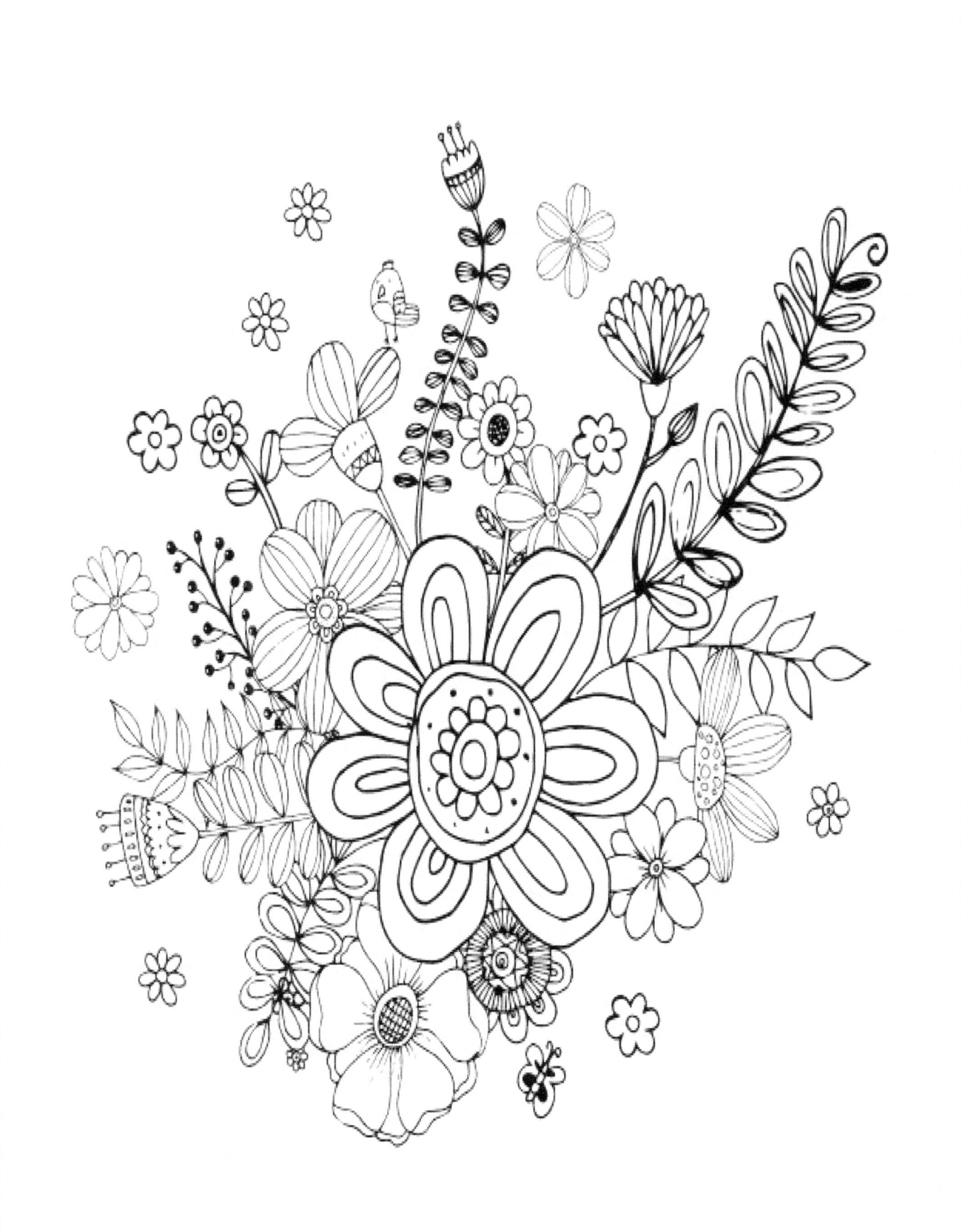

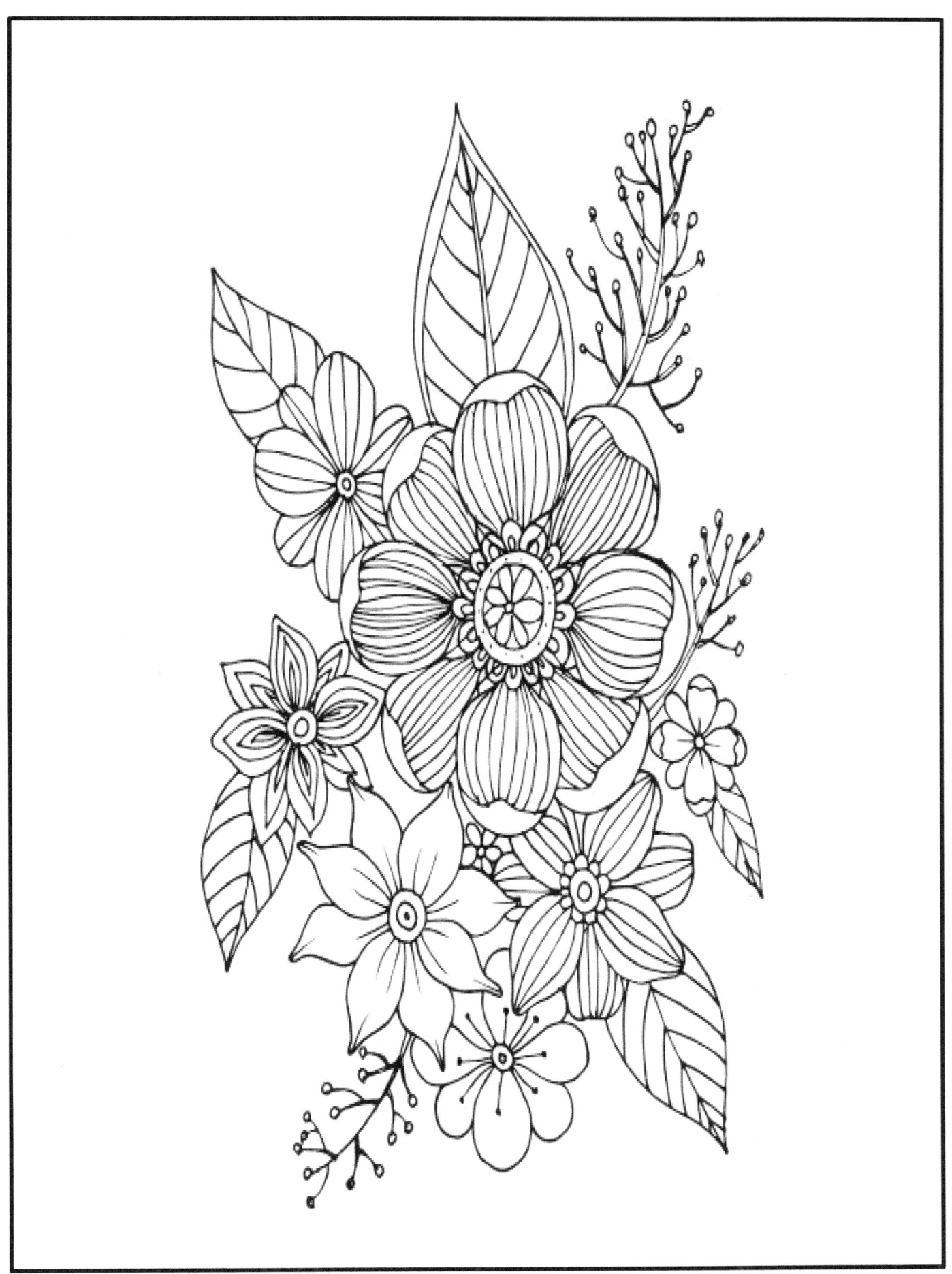

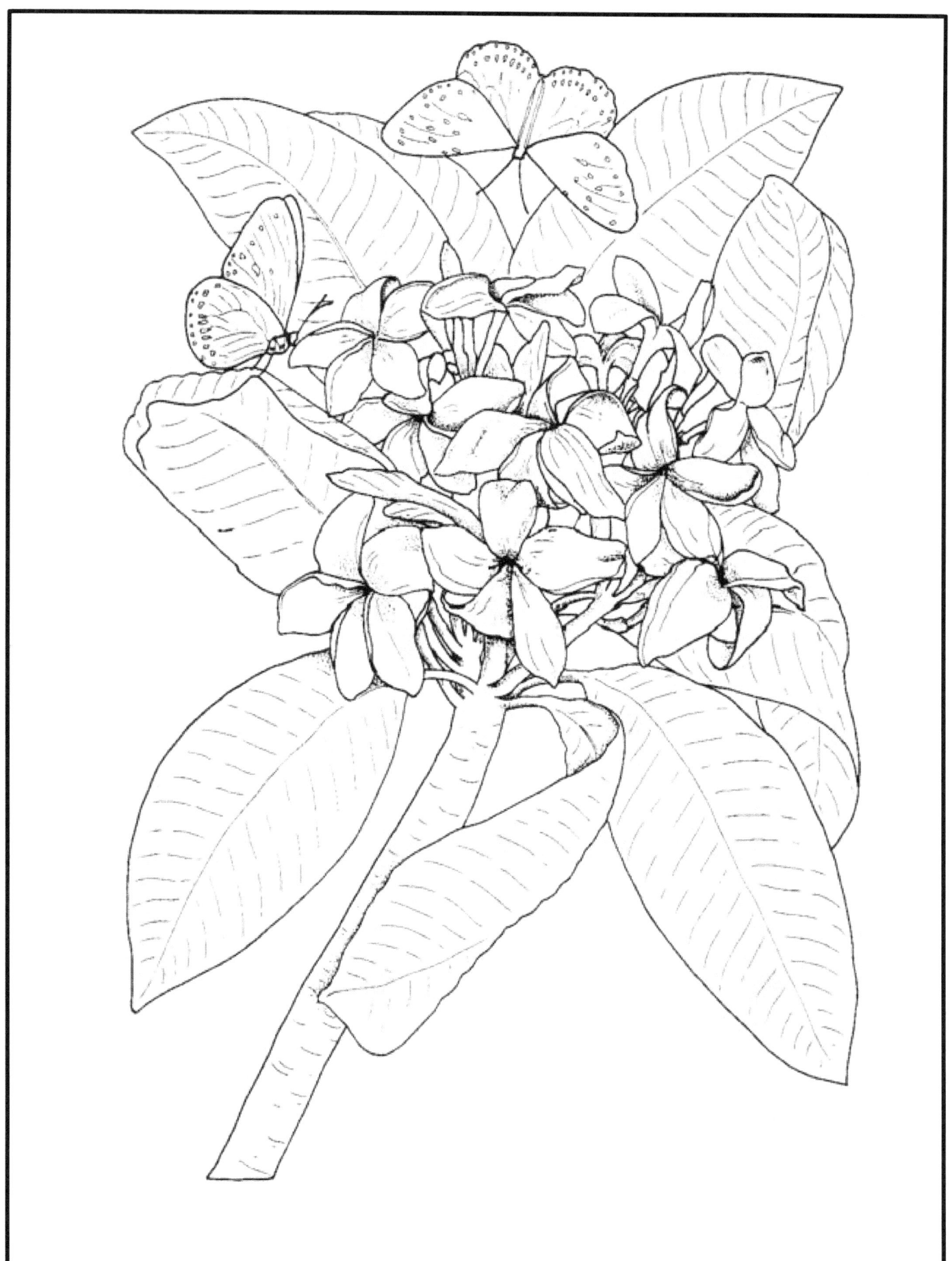

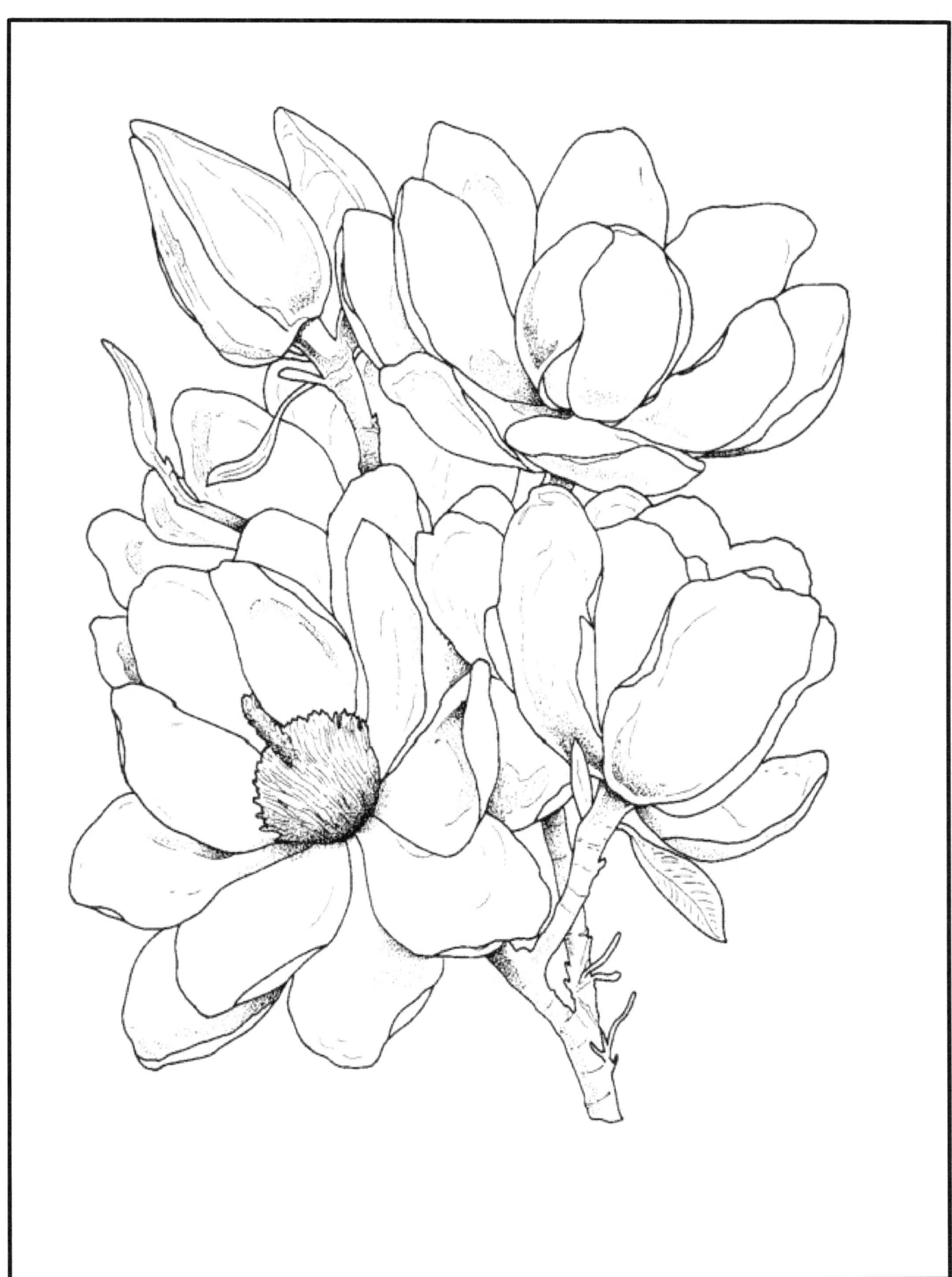

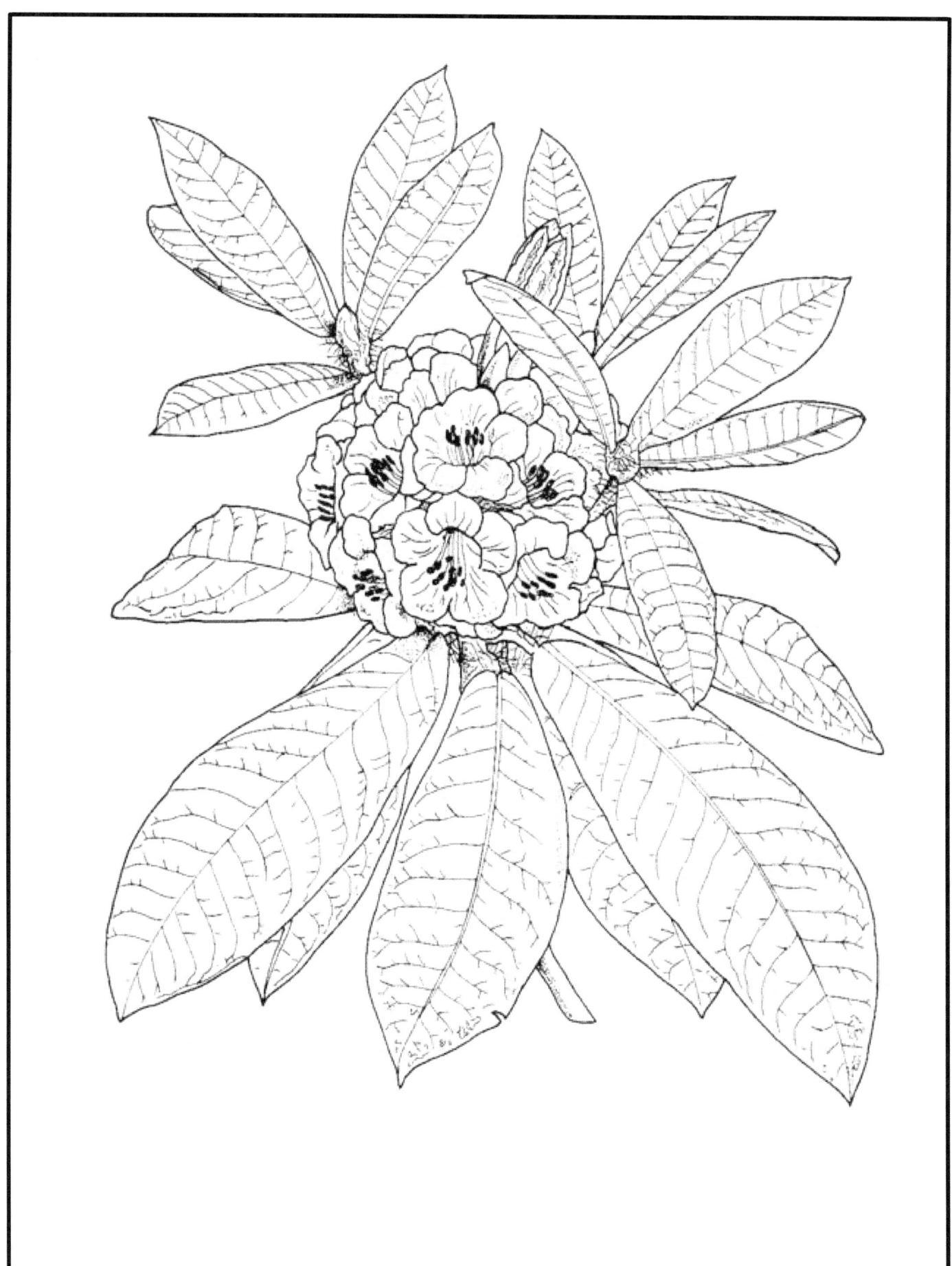

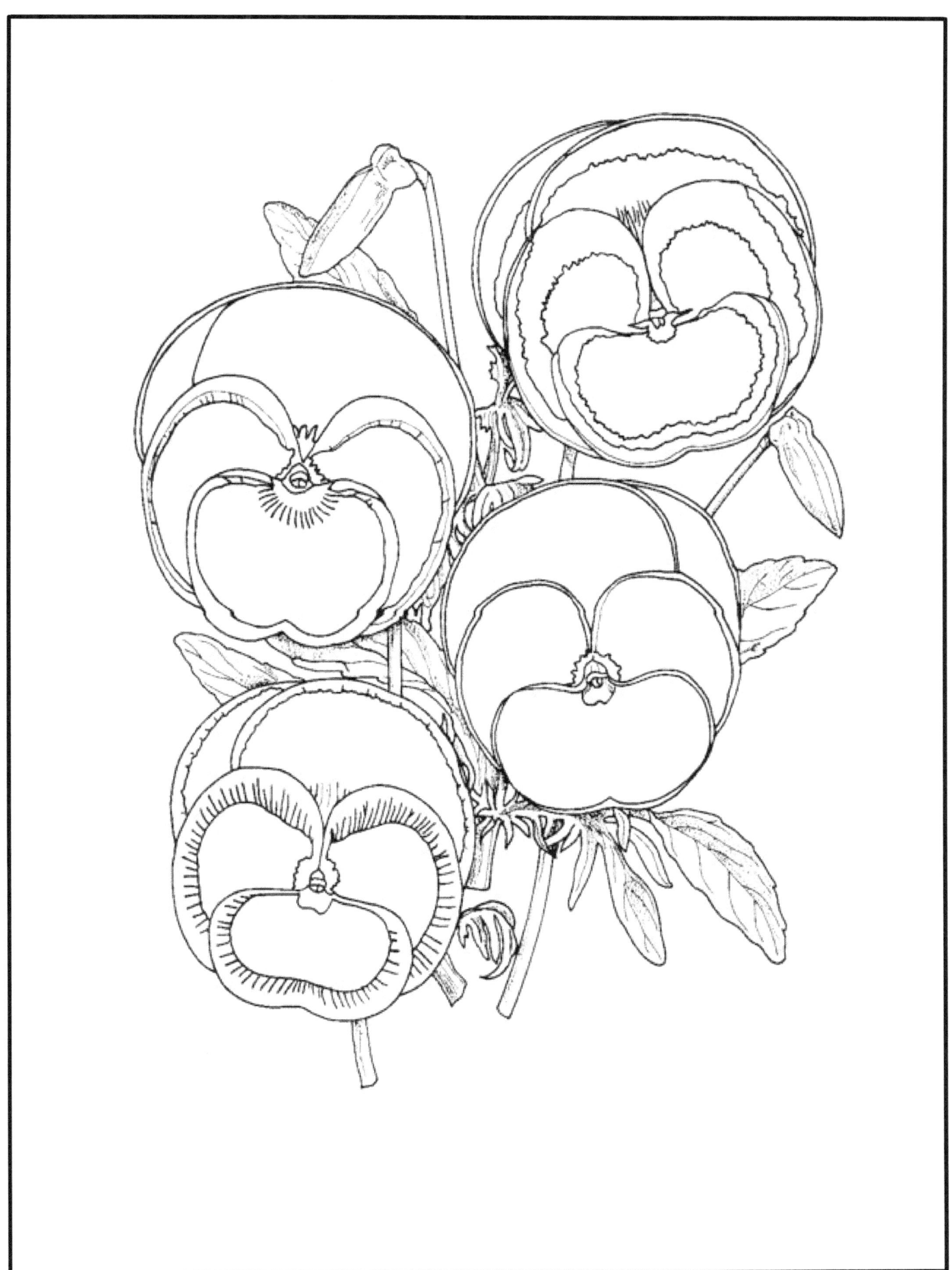

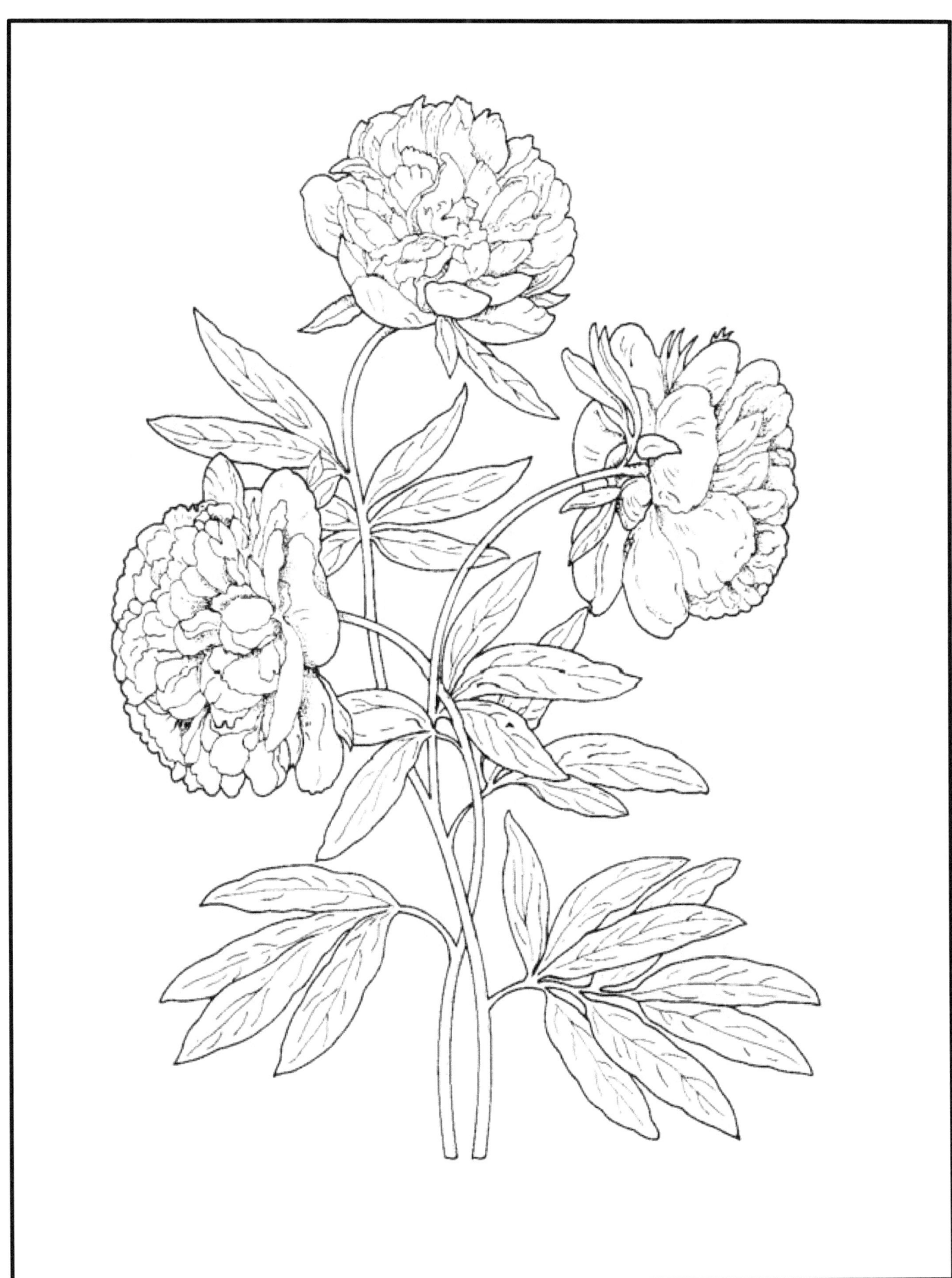

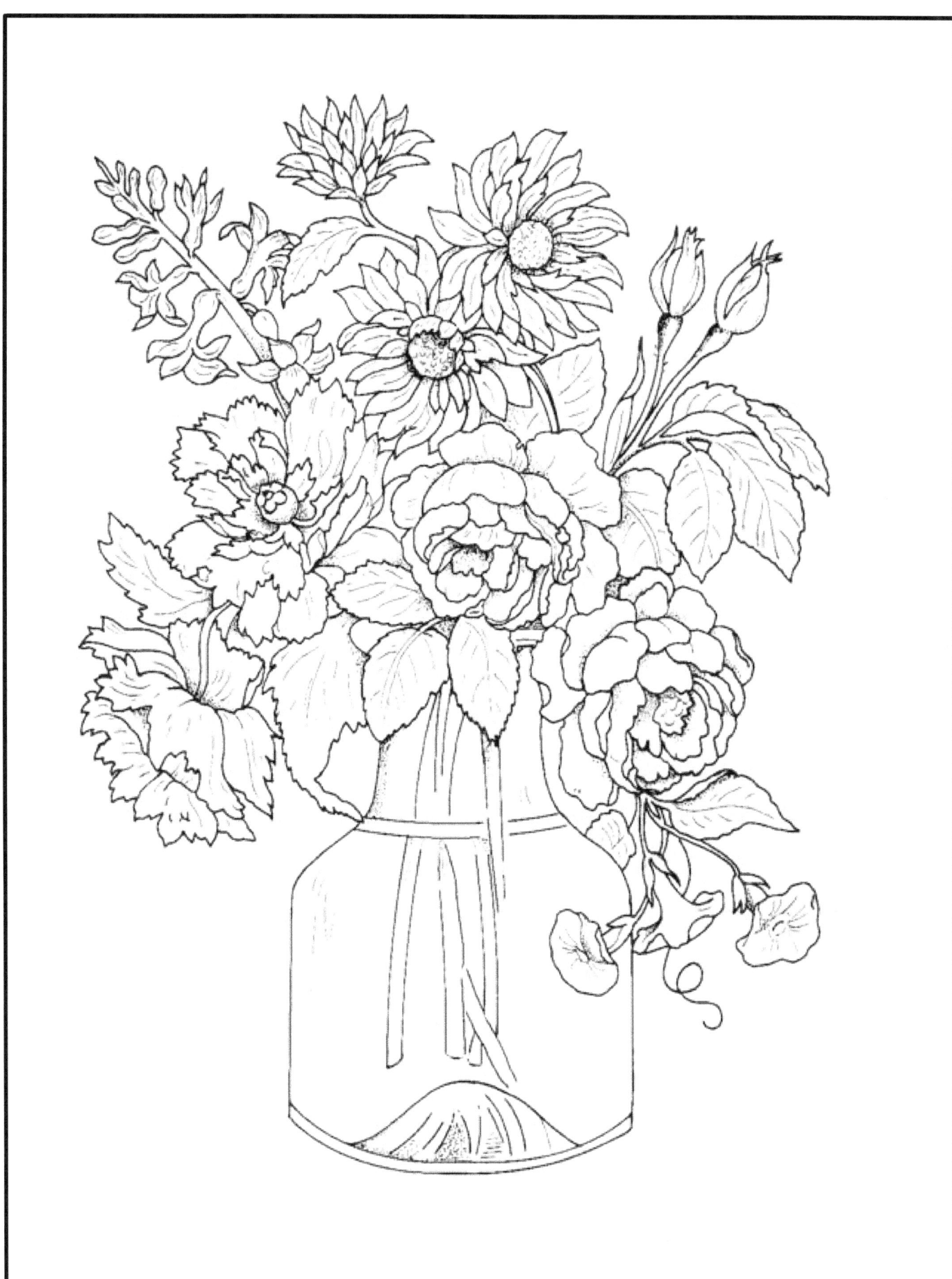

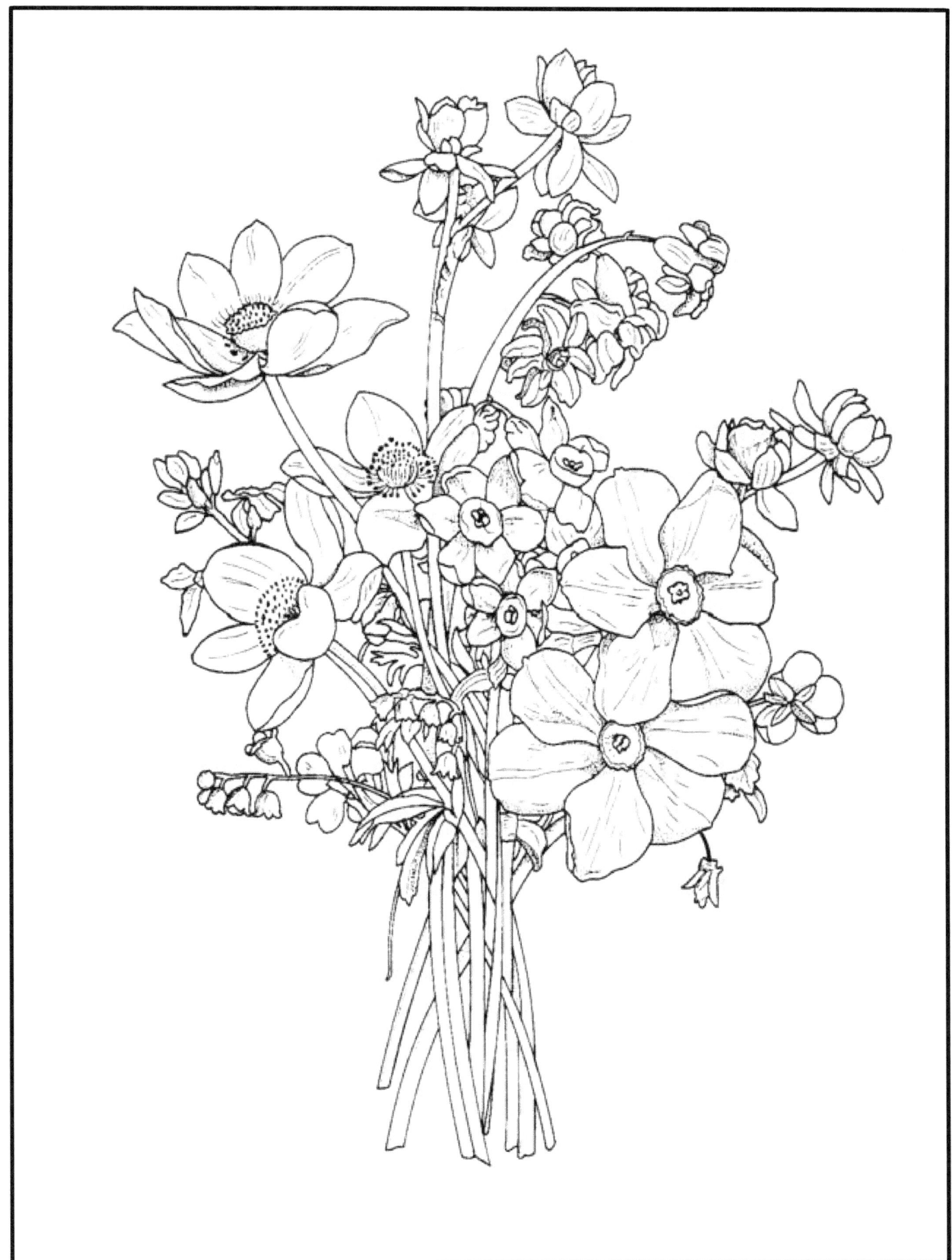

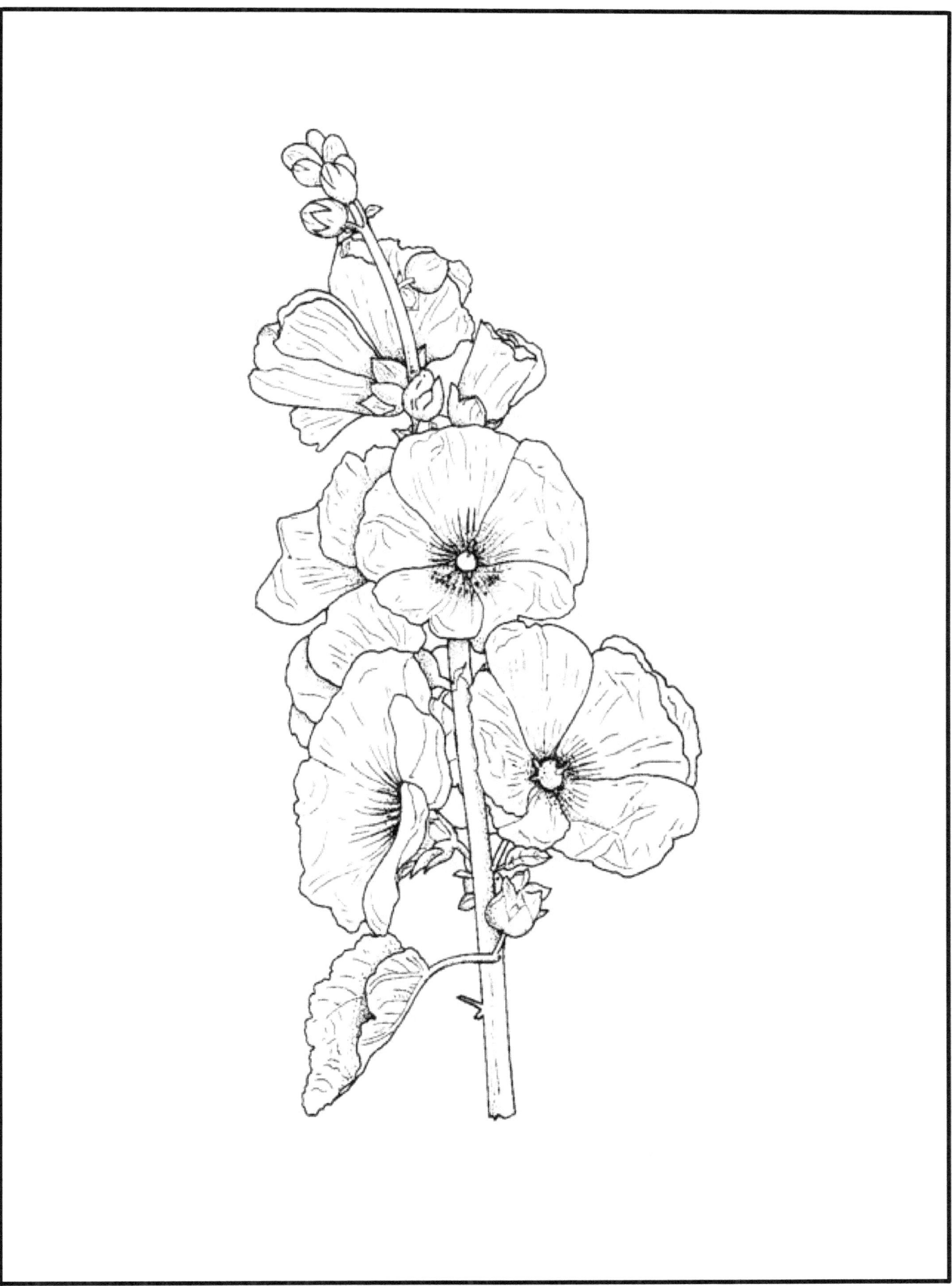

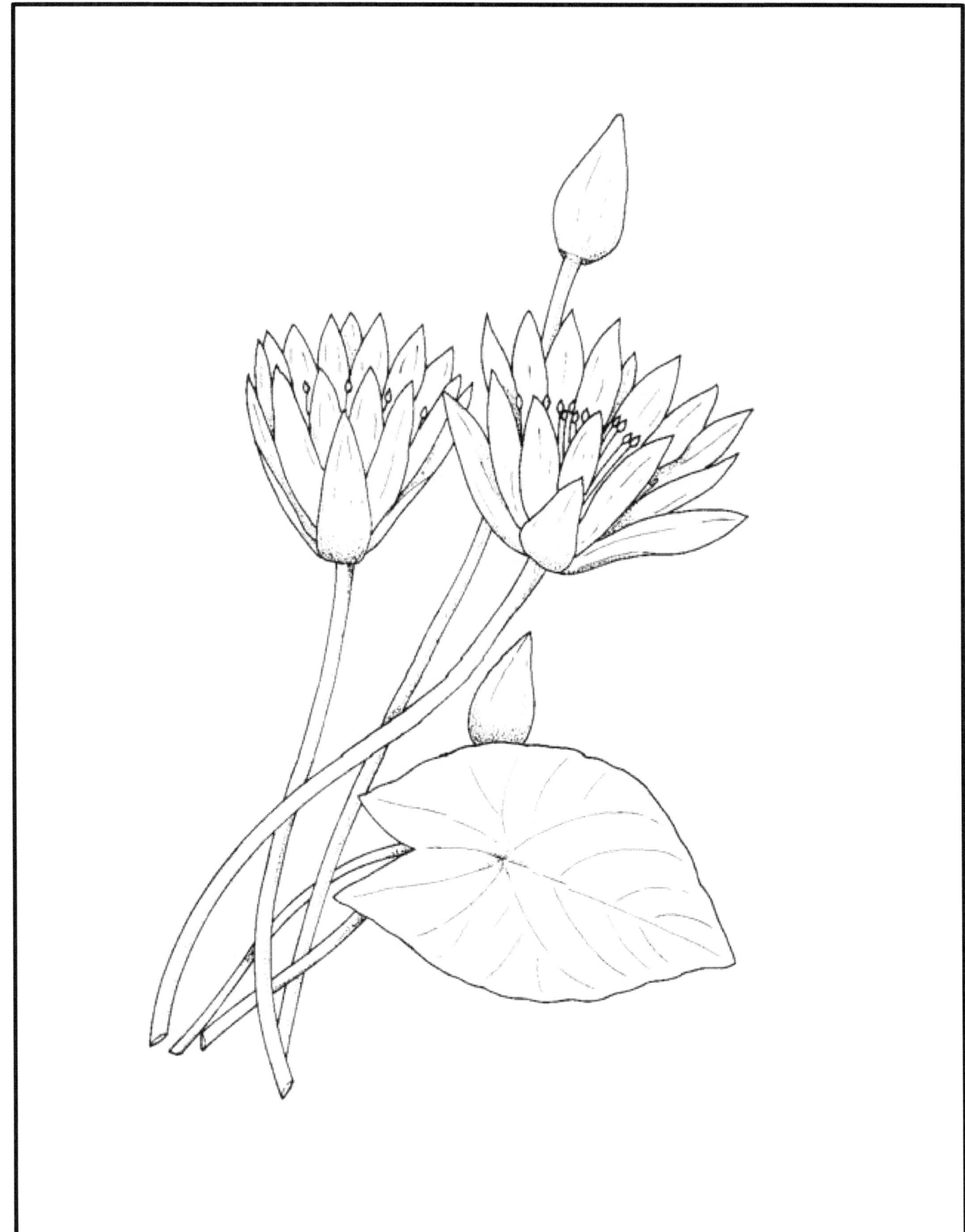

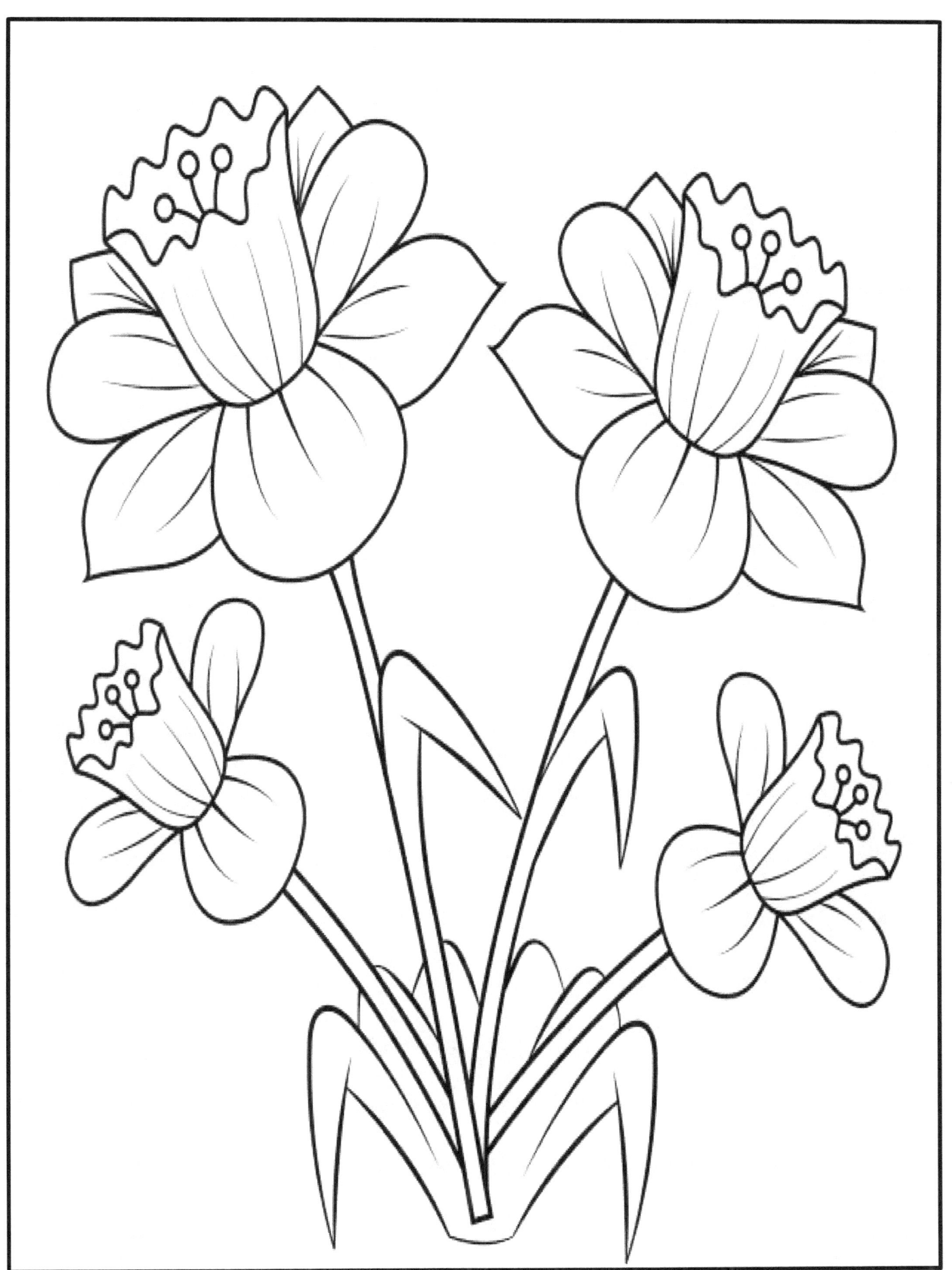

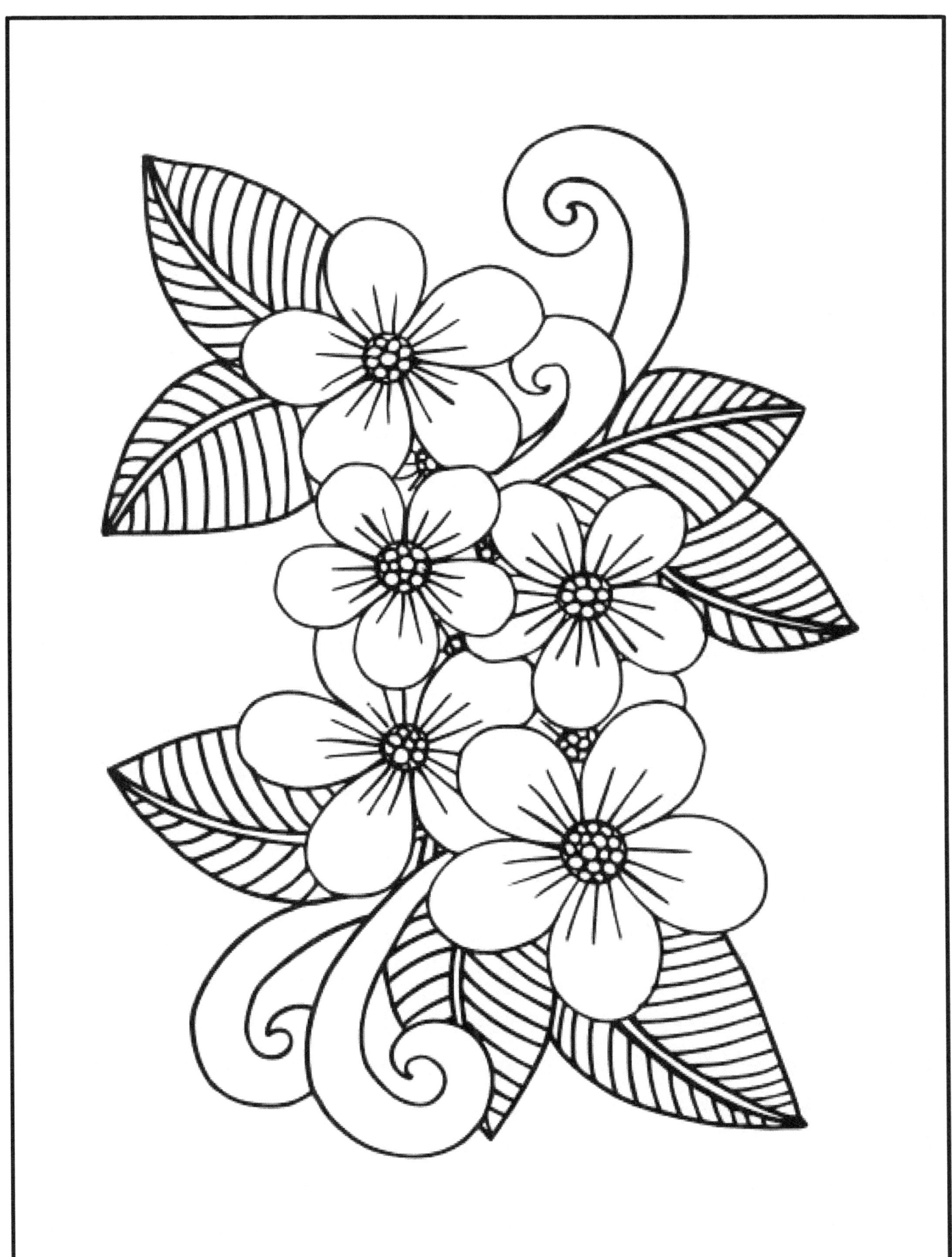

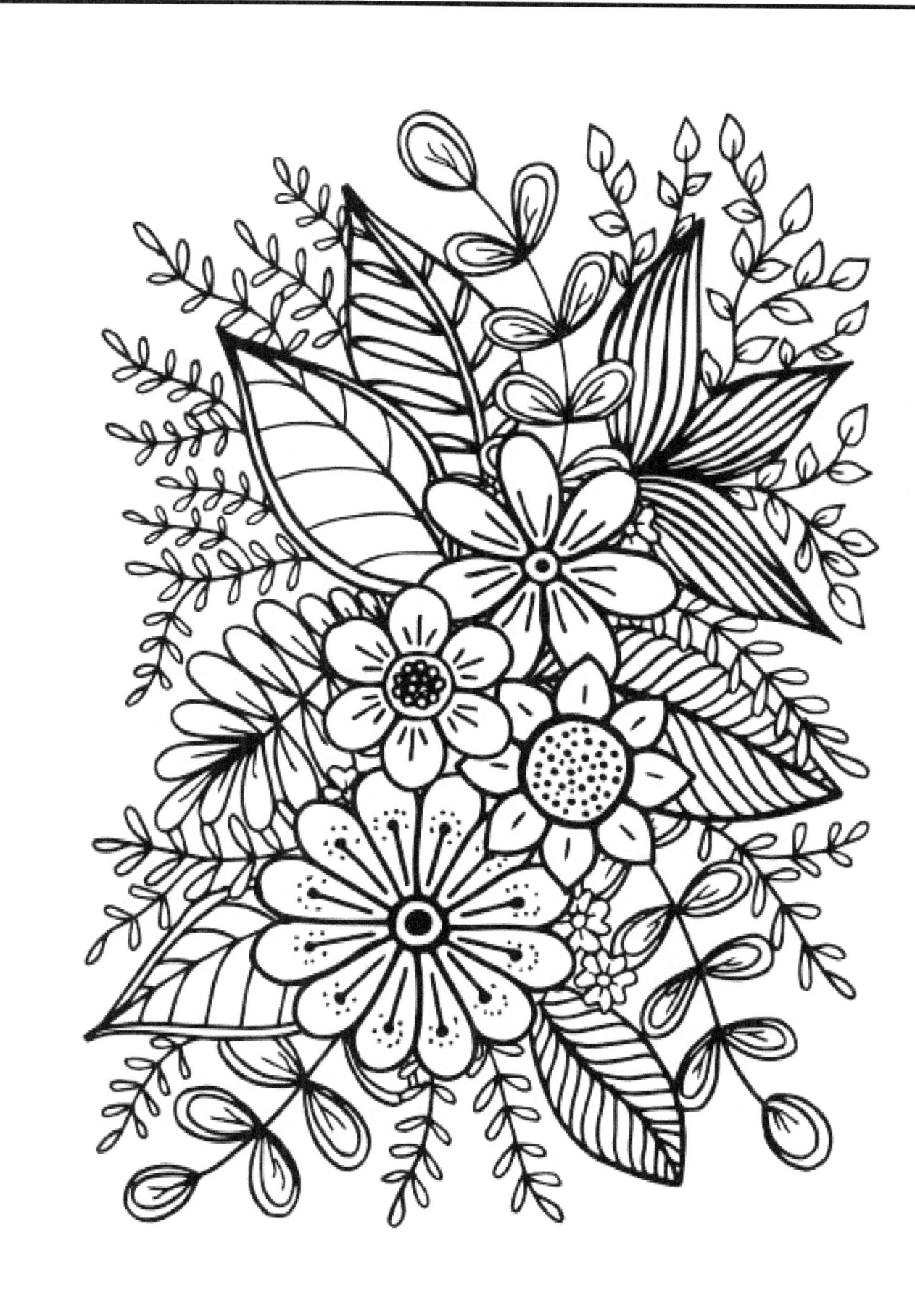

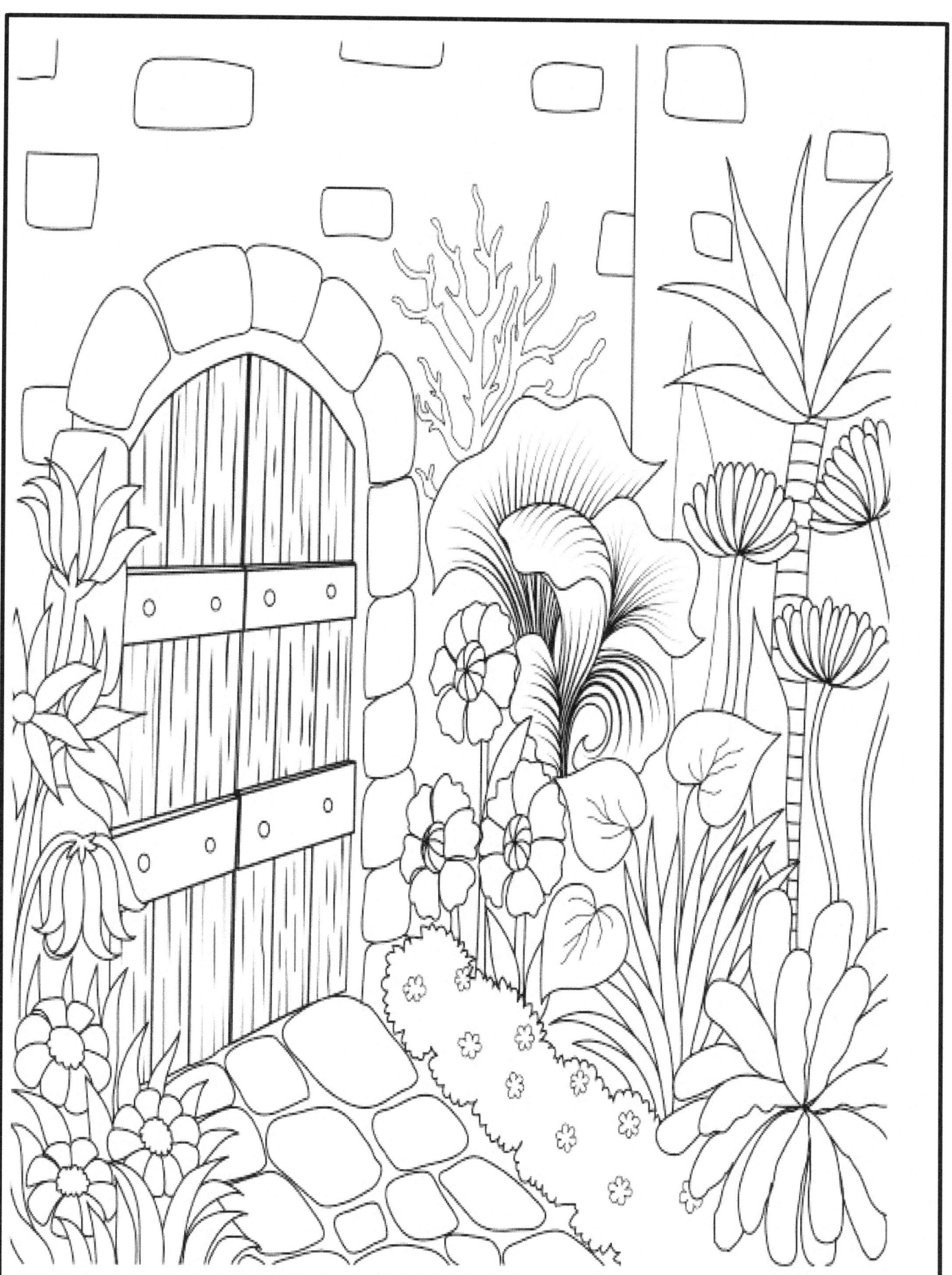

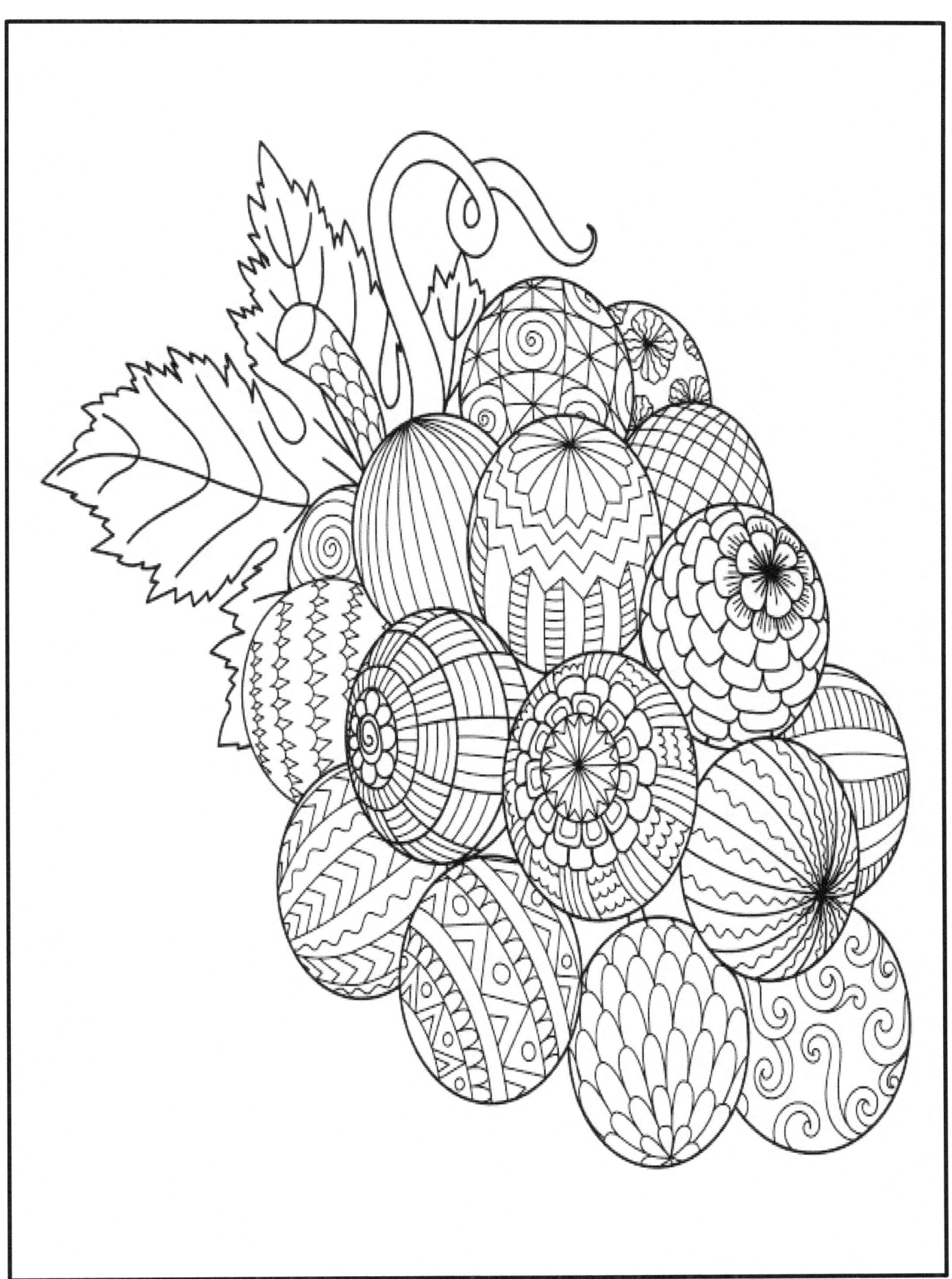

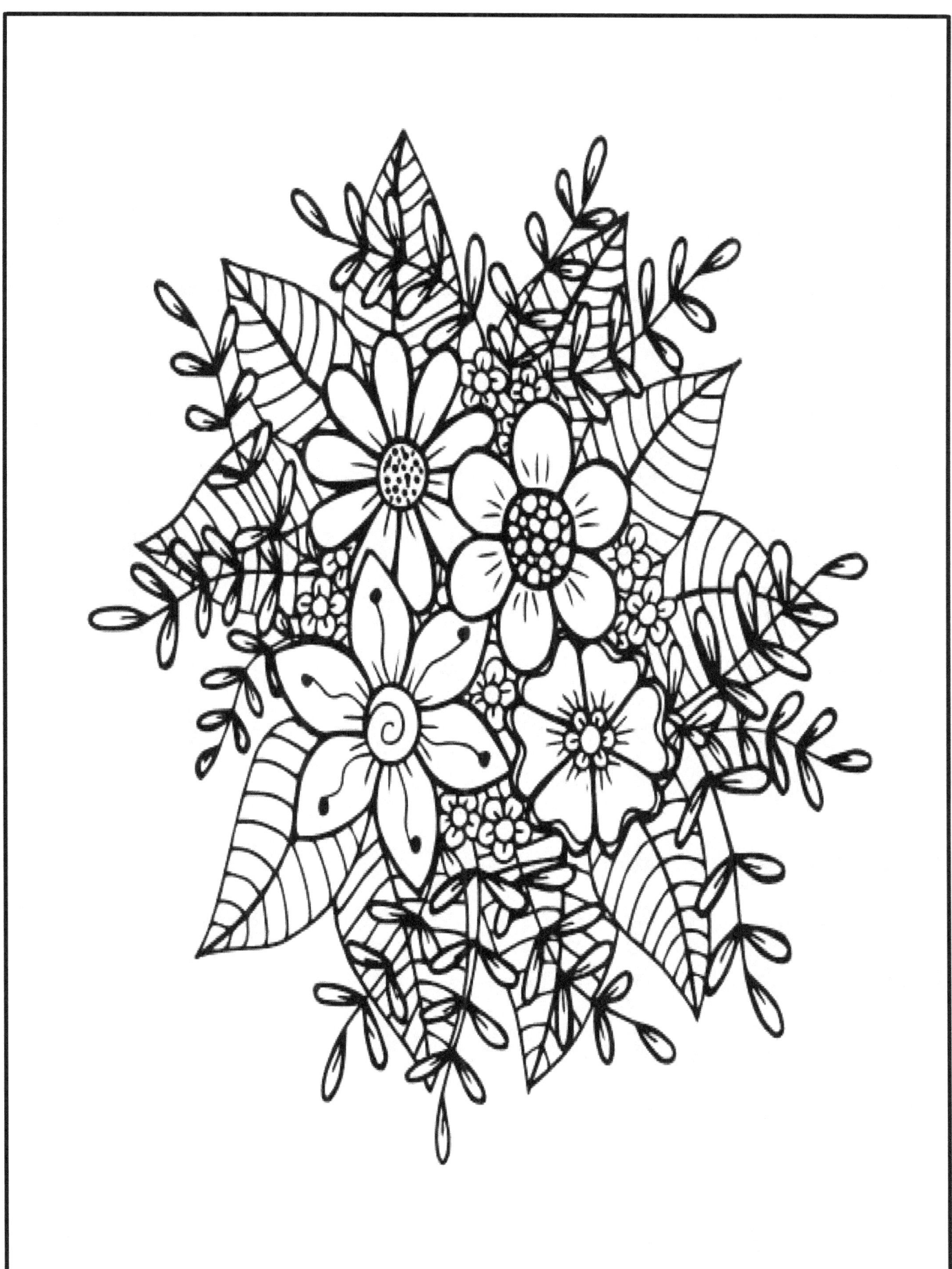

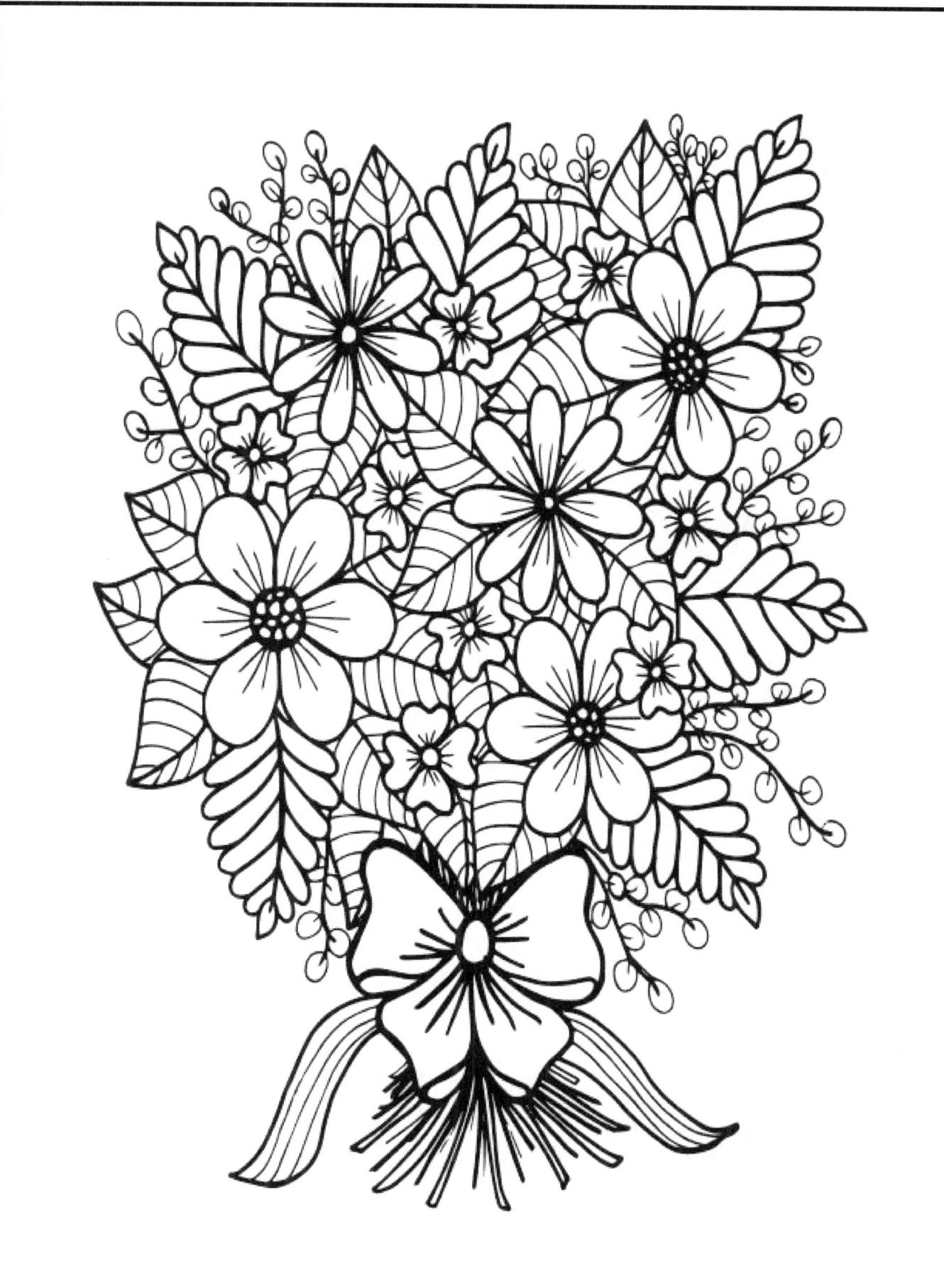

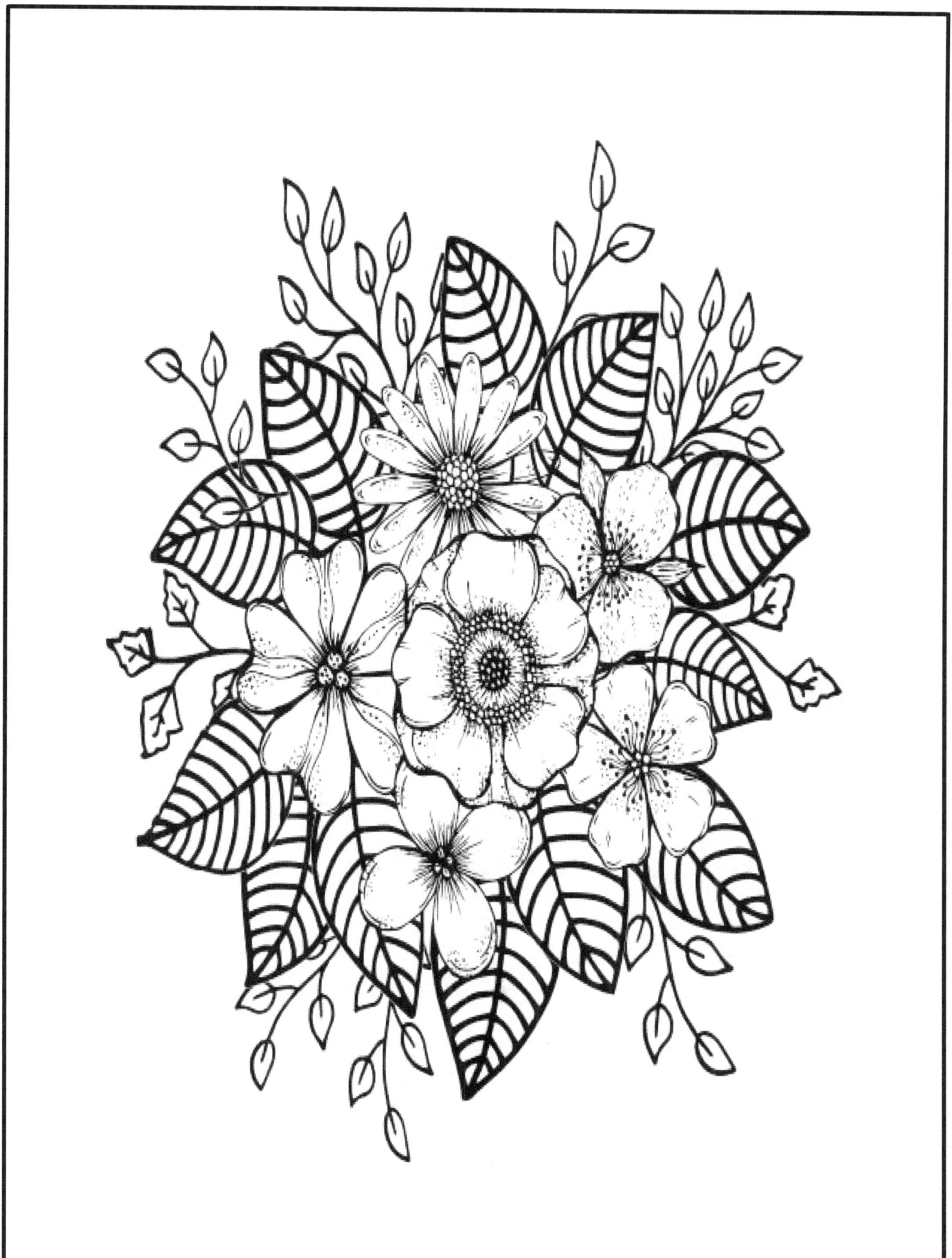

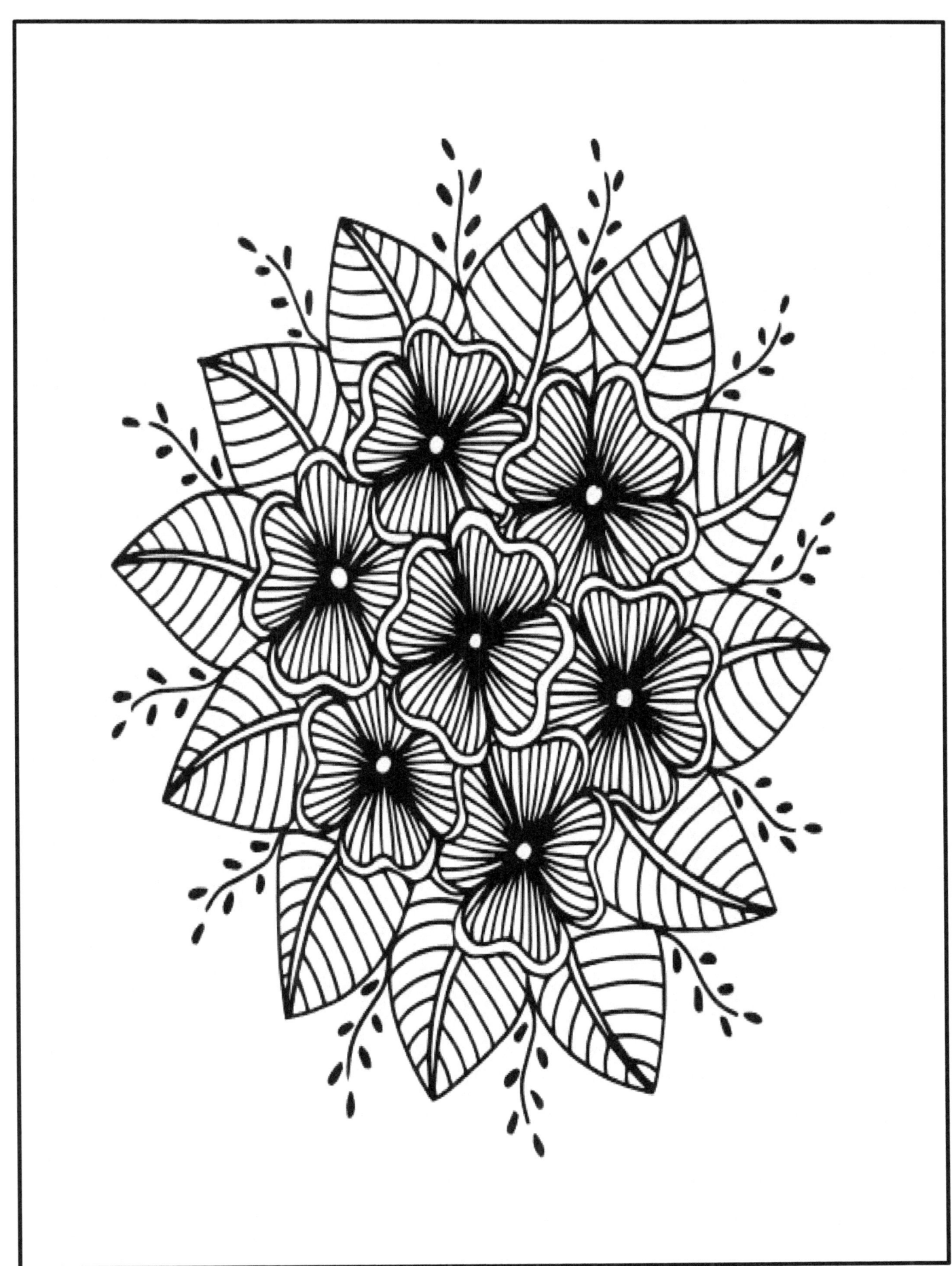

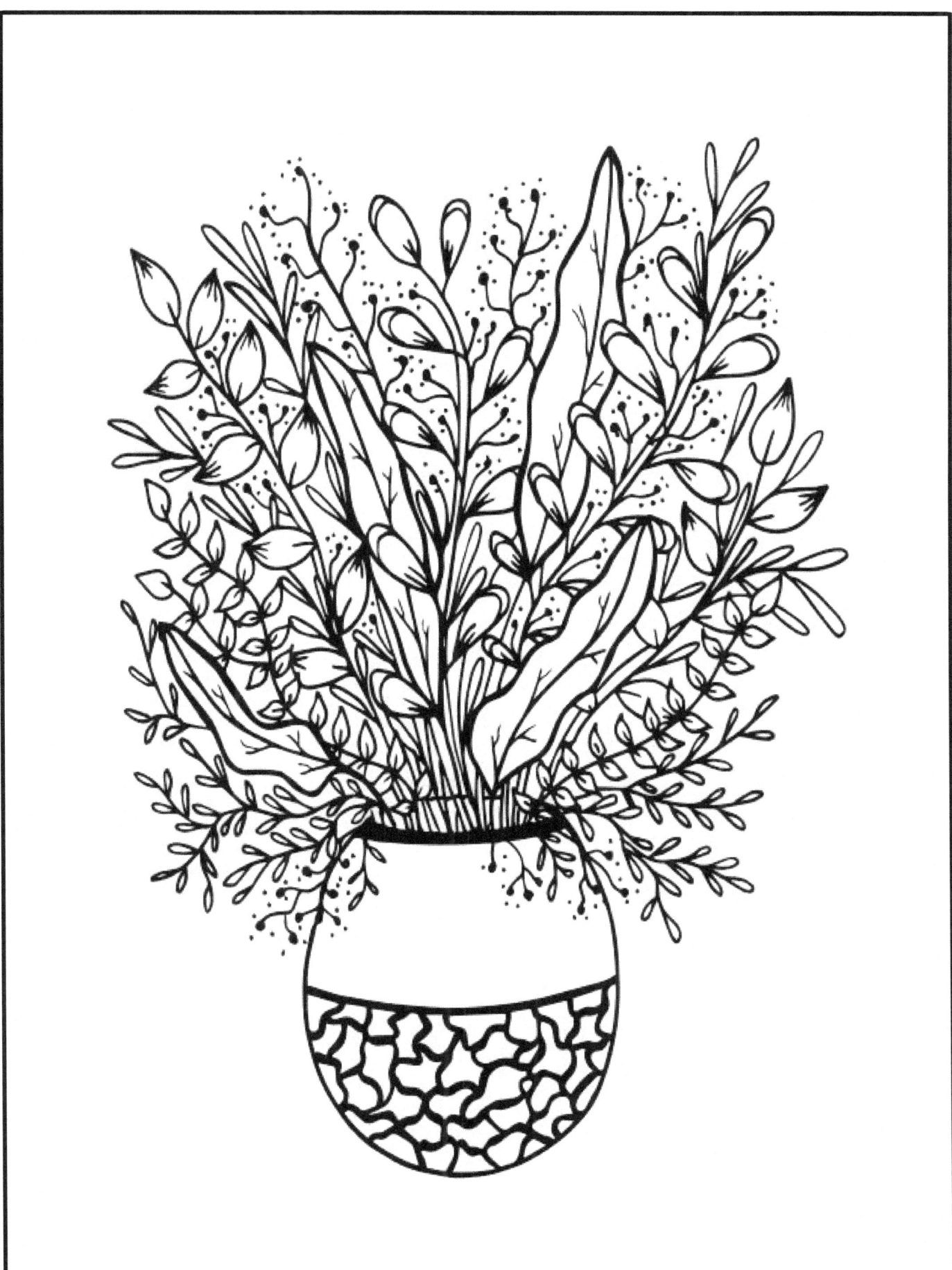

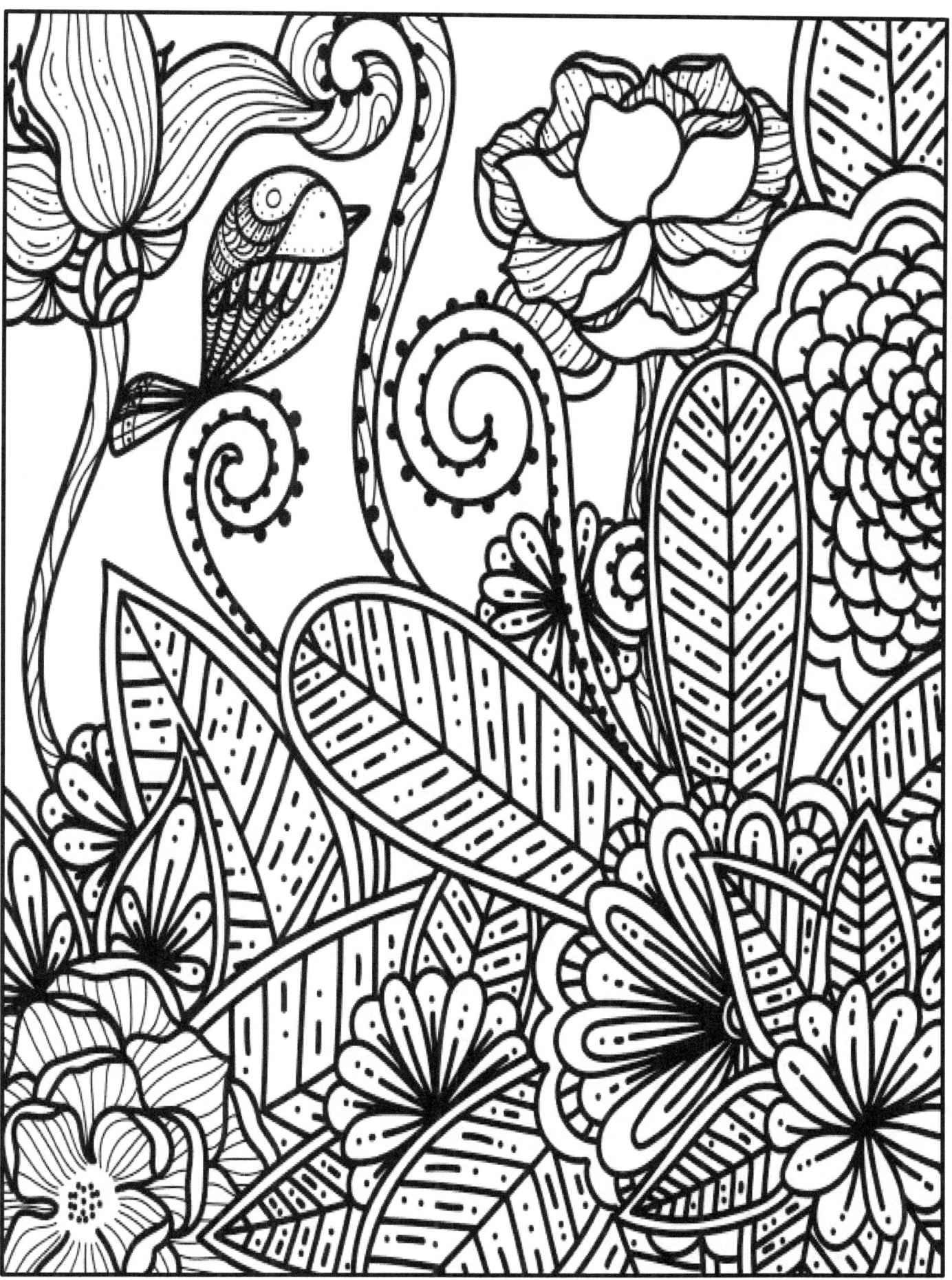

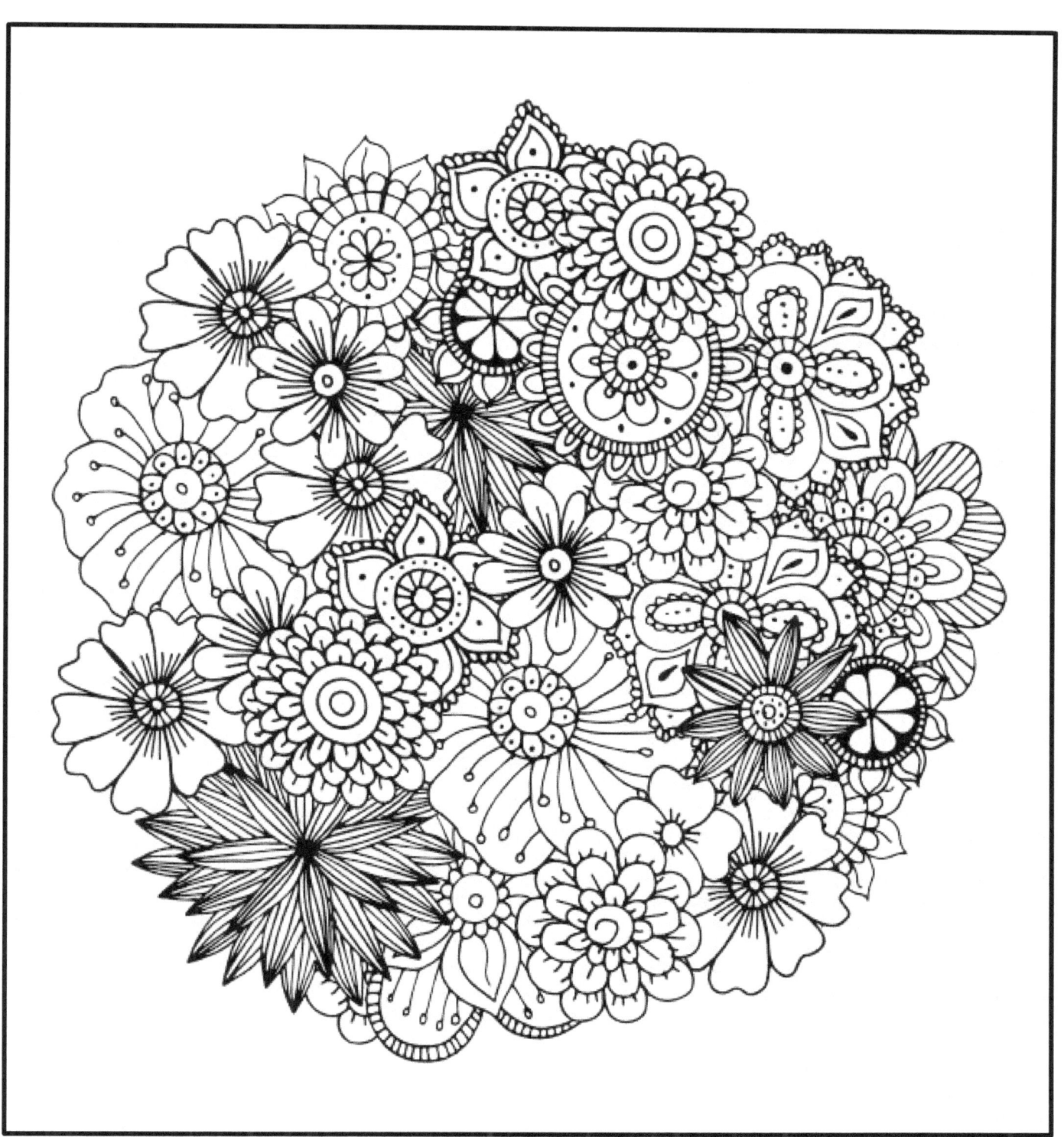

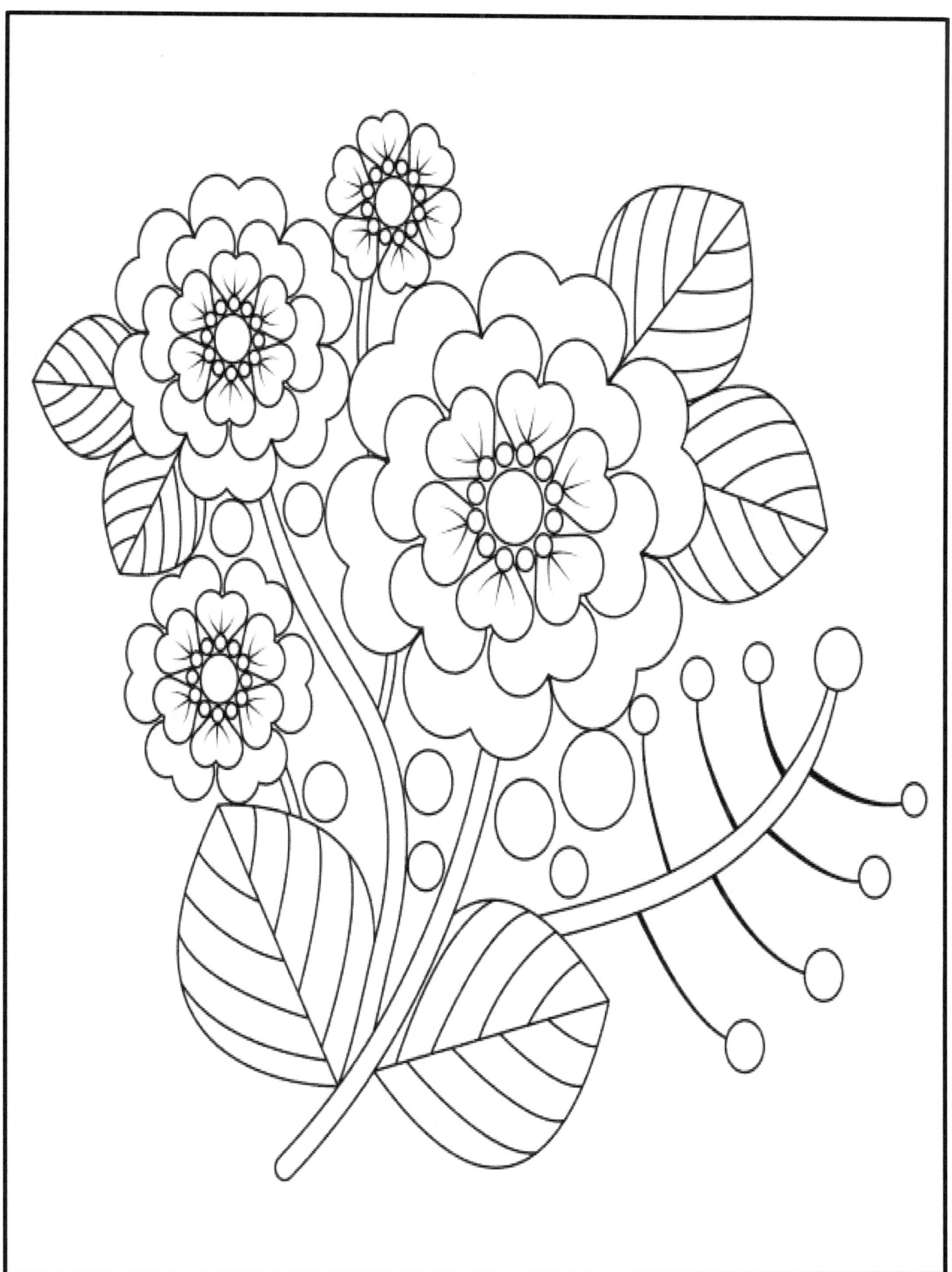

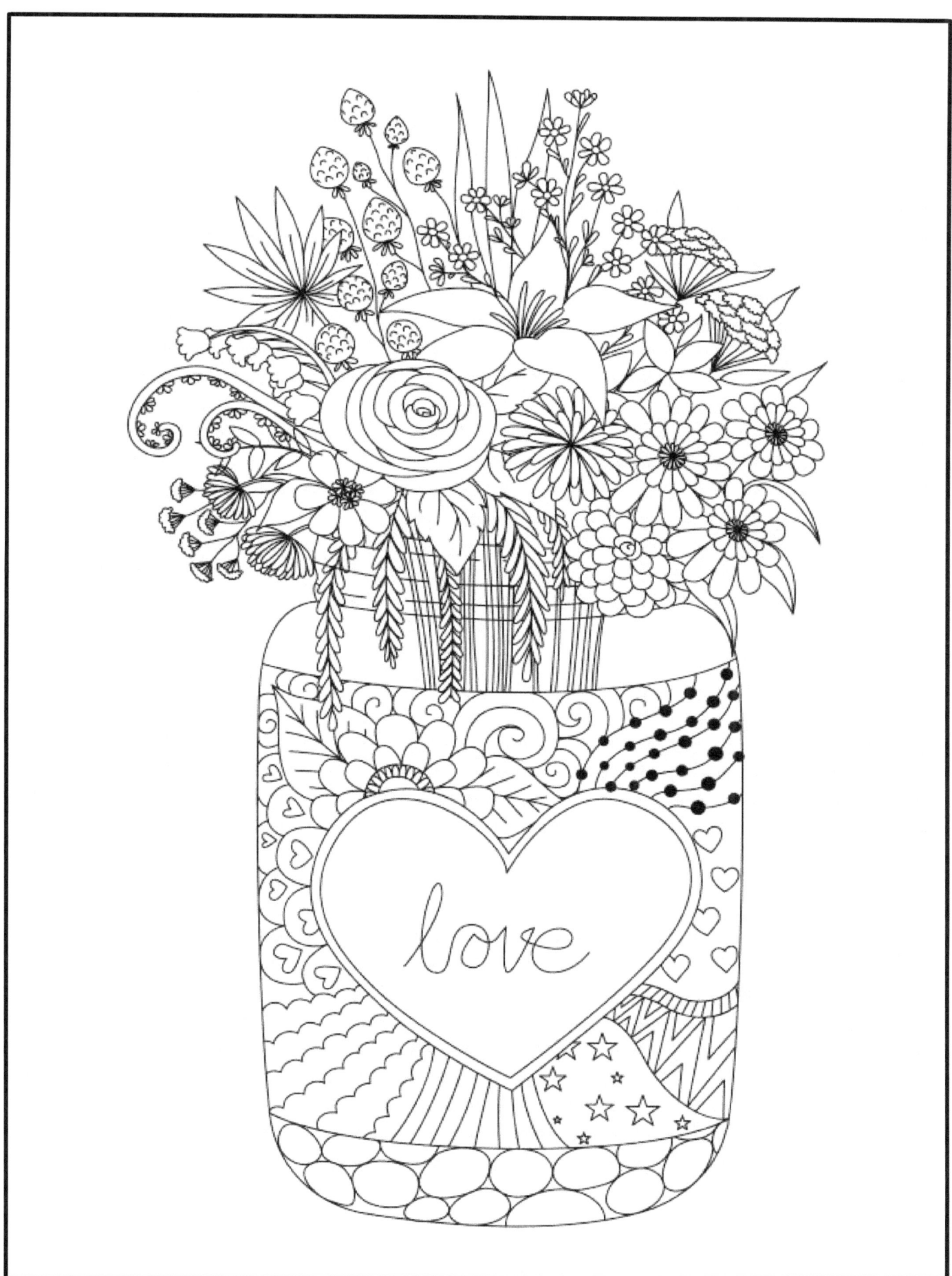

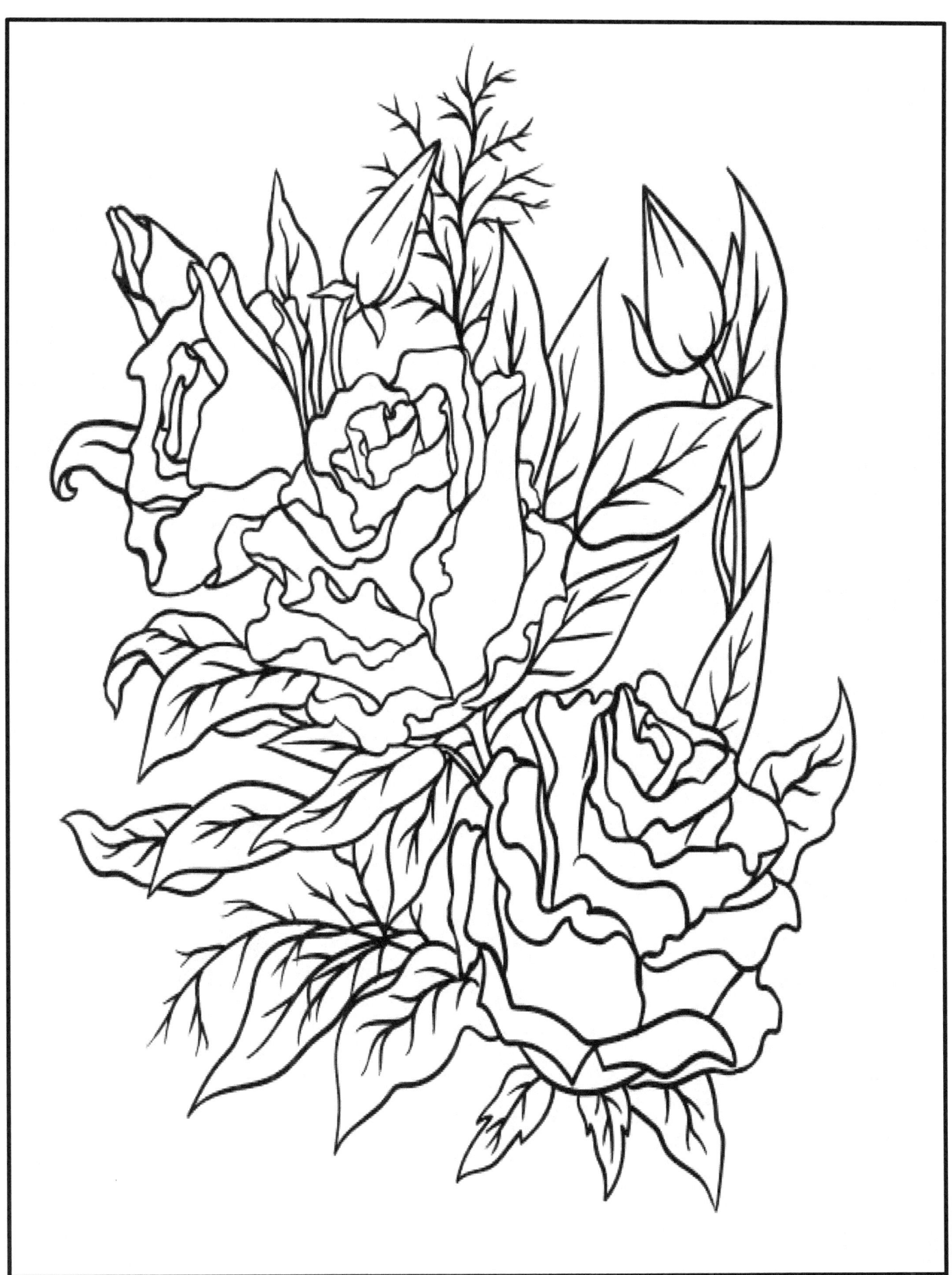

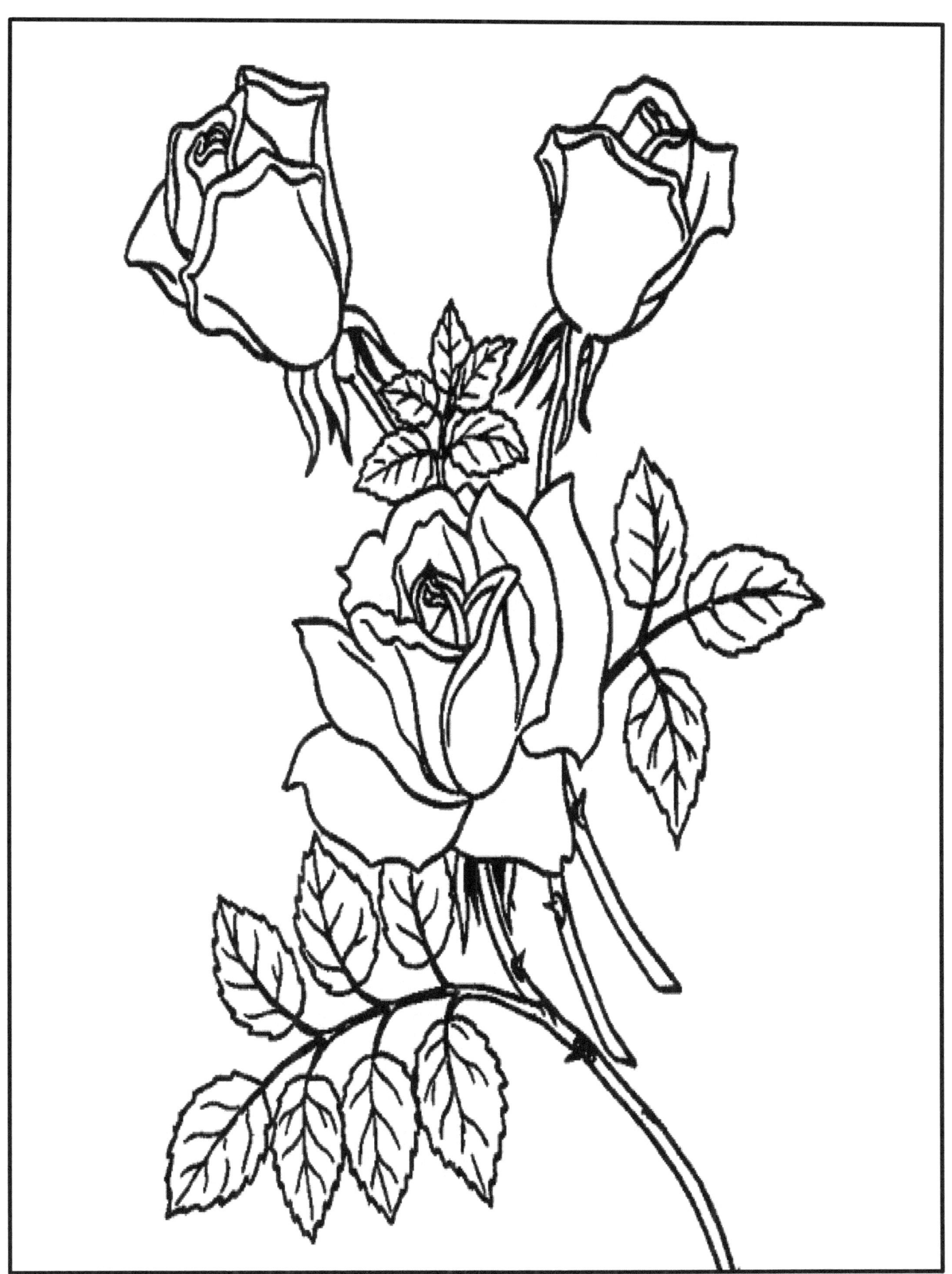

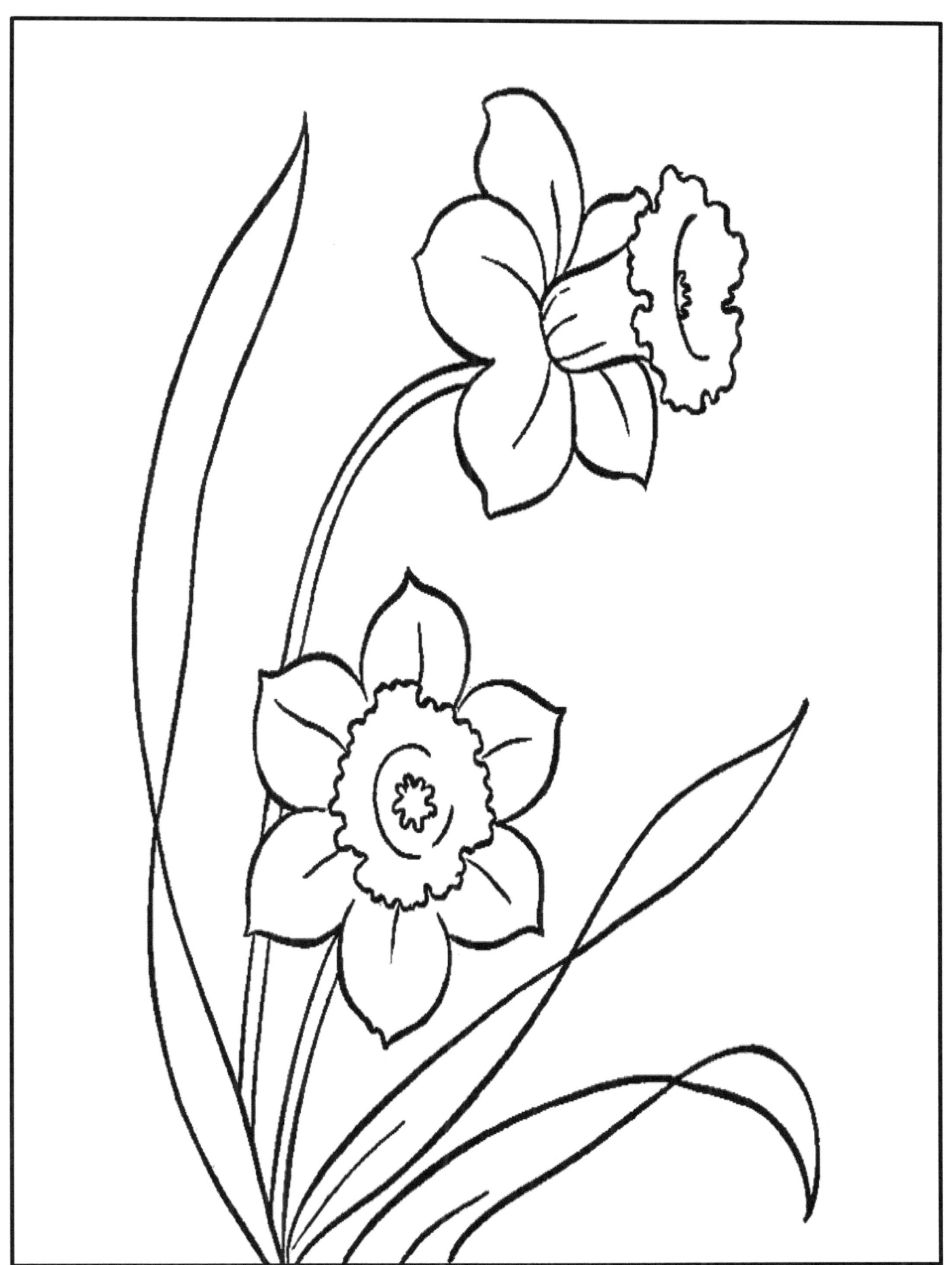

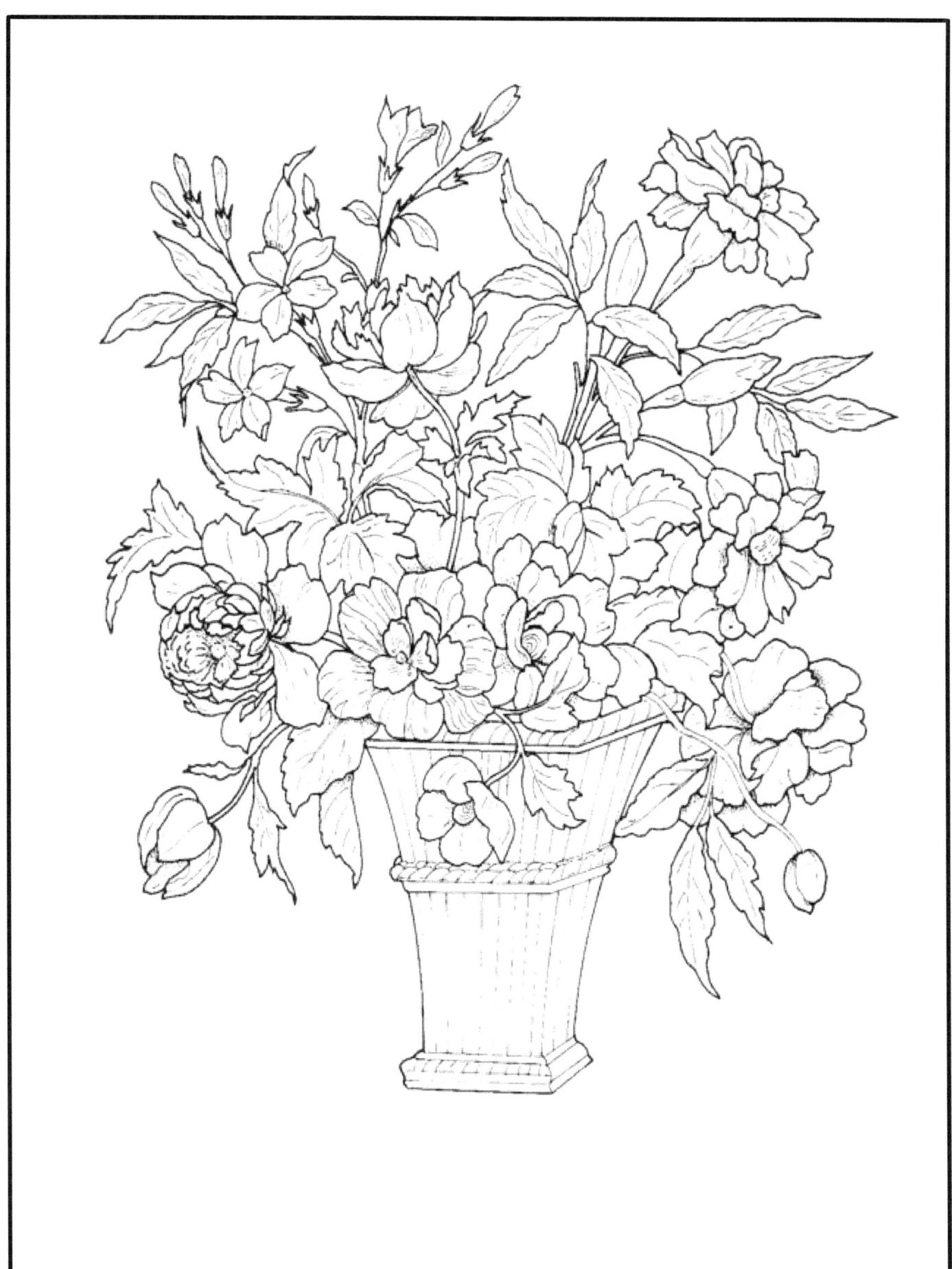

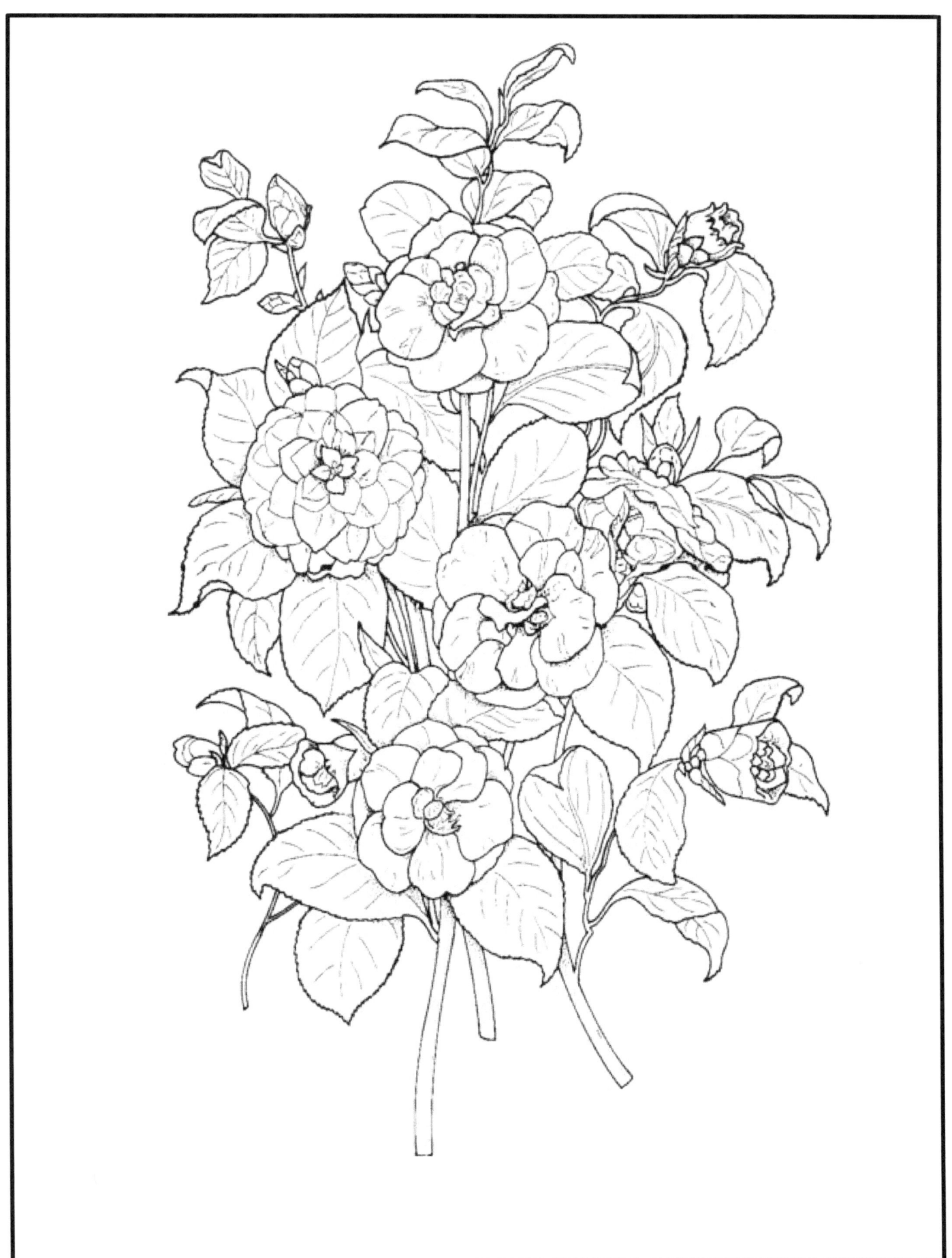

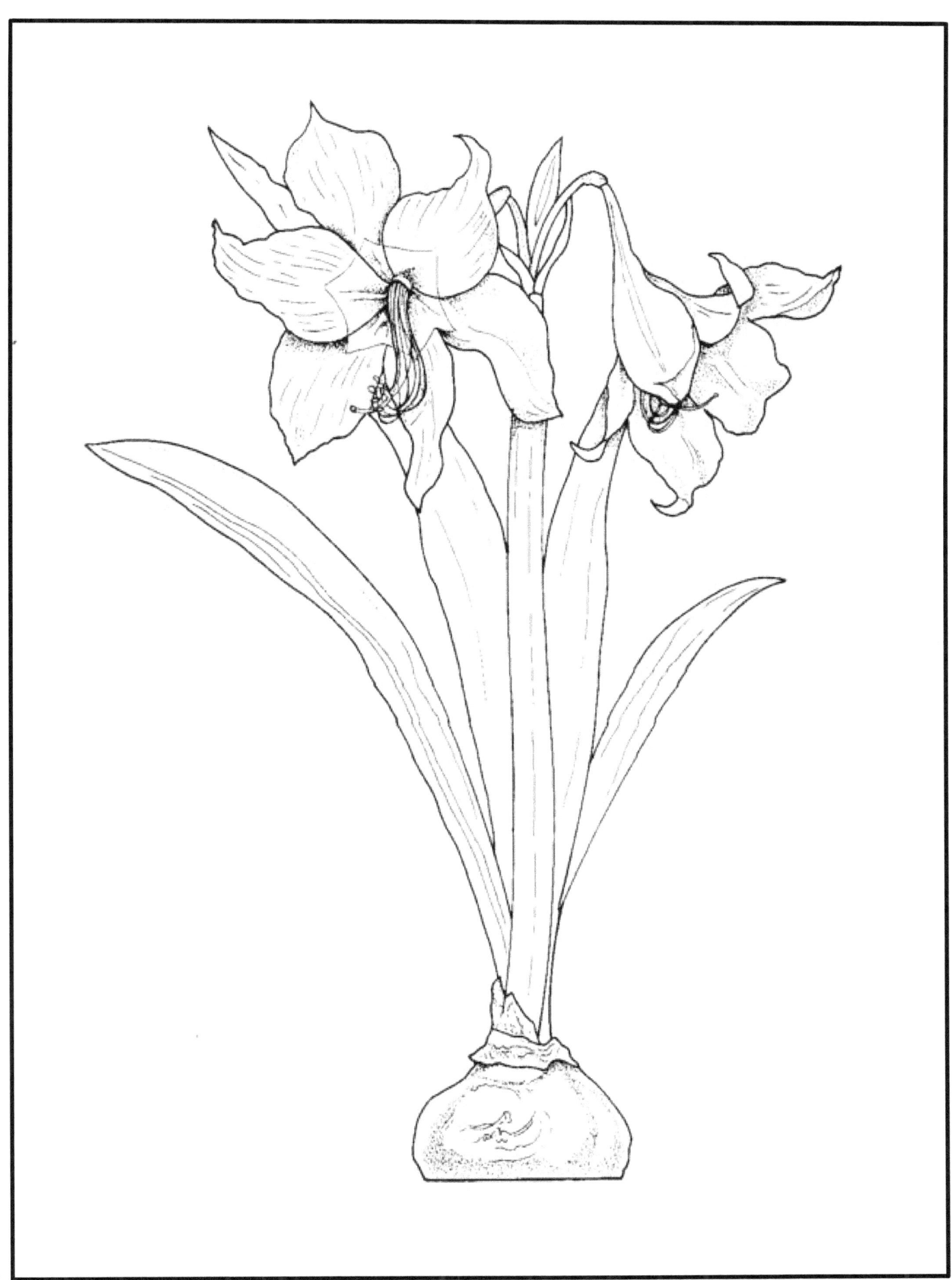

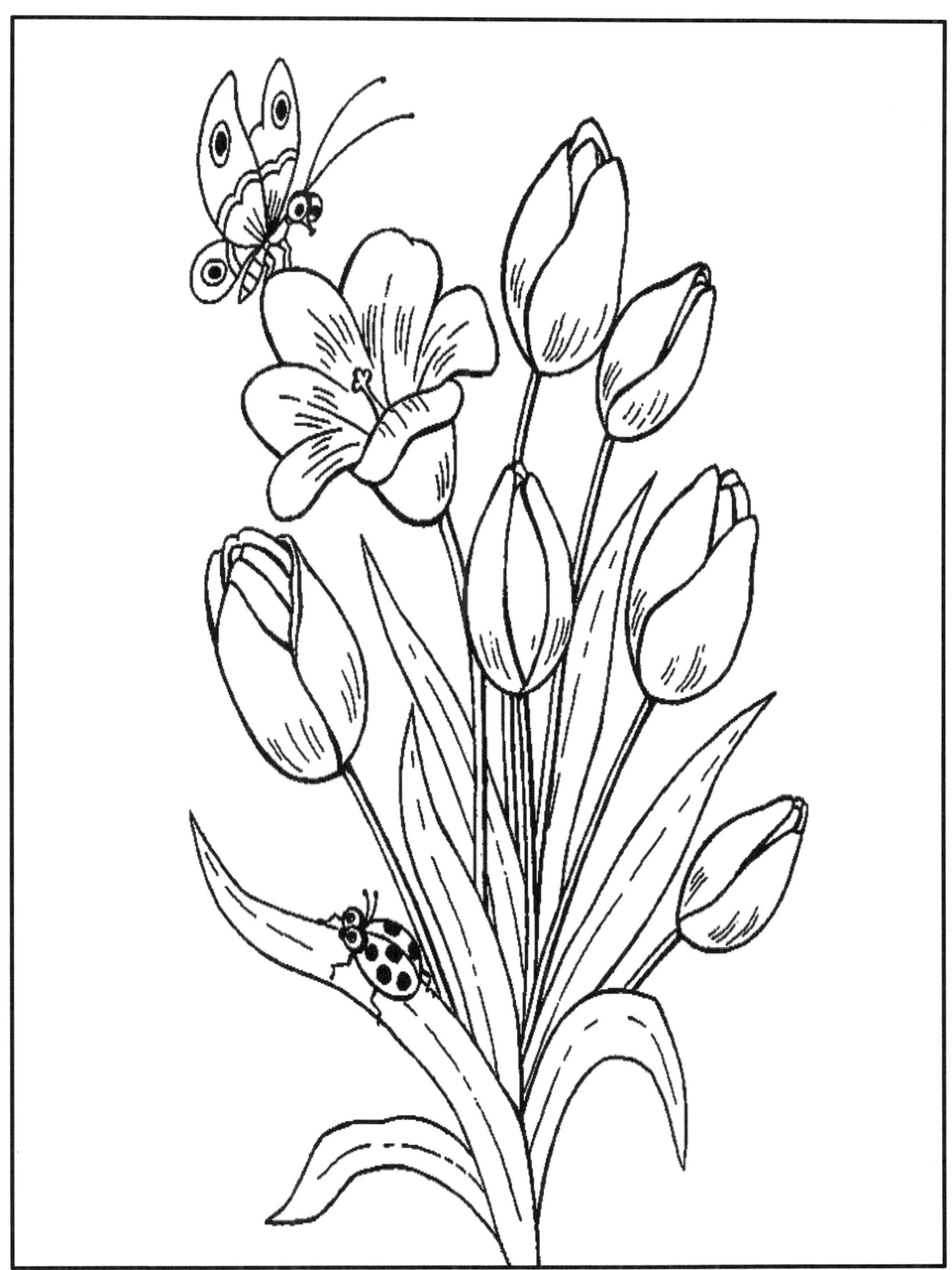

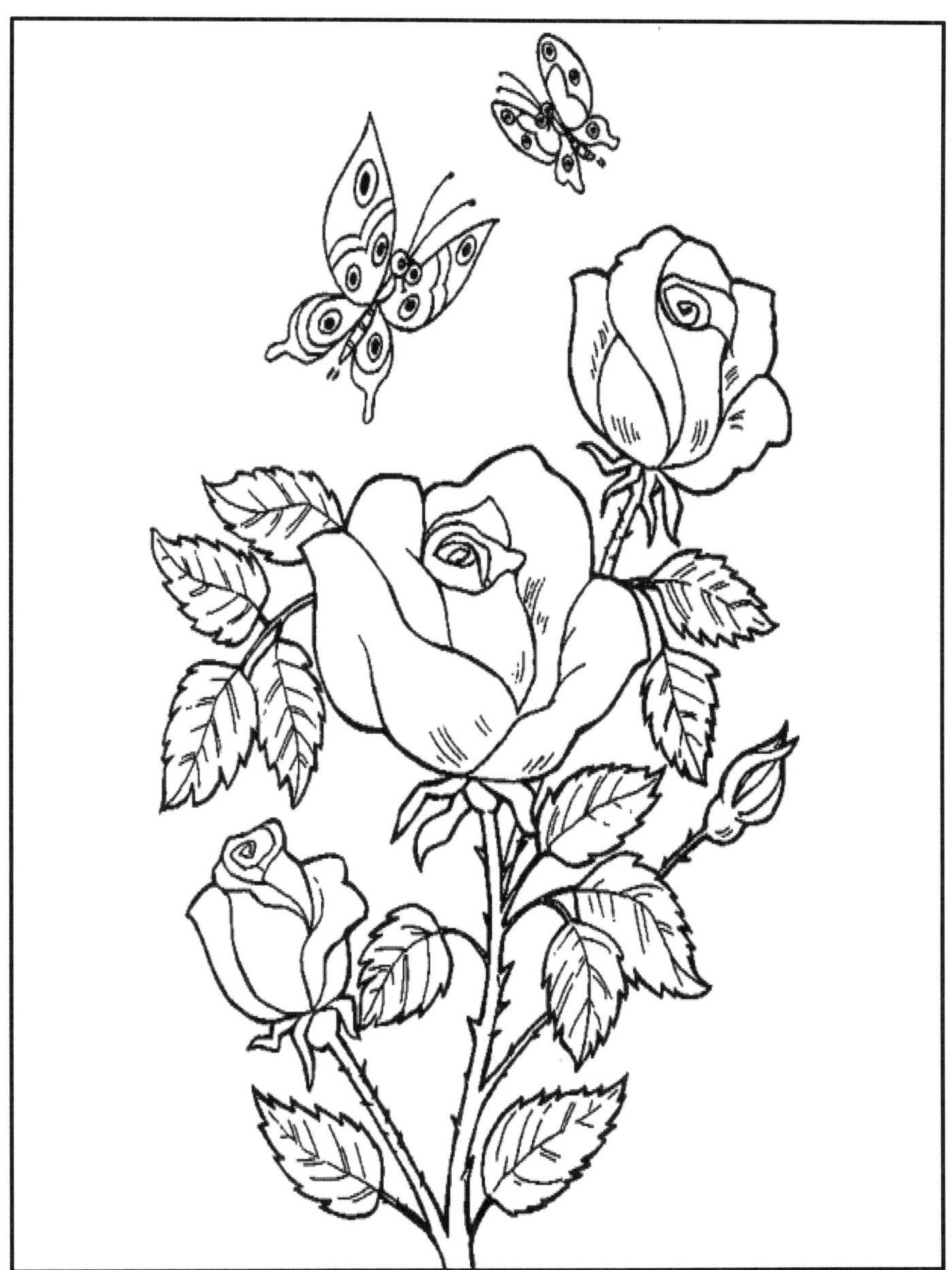

www.ingramcontent.com/pod-product-compliance
Lightning Source LLC
Chambersburg PA
CBHW080609220526
45466CB00010B/3295